THE LAKE DISTRICT OF MINNEAPOLIS

A History of the Calhoun-Isles Community

THE LAKE DISTRICT OF MINNEAPOLIS

A History of the Calhoun-Isles Community

David A. Lanegran

Ernest R. Sandeen

With the assistance of

Bonnie Richter

Valerie Stetson

Barbara Young

Living Historical Museum   St. Paul, Minnesota

A fisherman with four boys on the west shore of Cedar Lake in the 1890s (Minneapolis Public Library).

Additional copies of this book or of *St. Paul's Historic Summit Avenue*,
published by the Living Historical Museum in 1978, may be ordered from

Living Historical Museum
826 Goodrich Avenue
St. Paul, MN 55105

Library of Congress Catalog Card Number: 79-84547

ISBN 0-933960-02-6 (Paper)

ISBN 0-933960-03-4 (Cloth)

Third printing 1981

Research for this book was carried out with funds provided by a grant from the Fifth Northwestern National Bank, Minneapolis, in commemoration of the bank's fiftieth year of service to the Calhoun-Isles community.

Contents

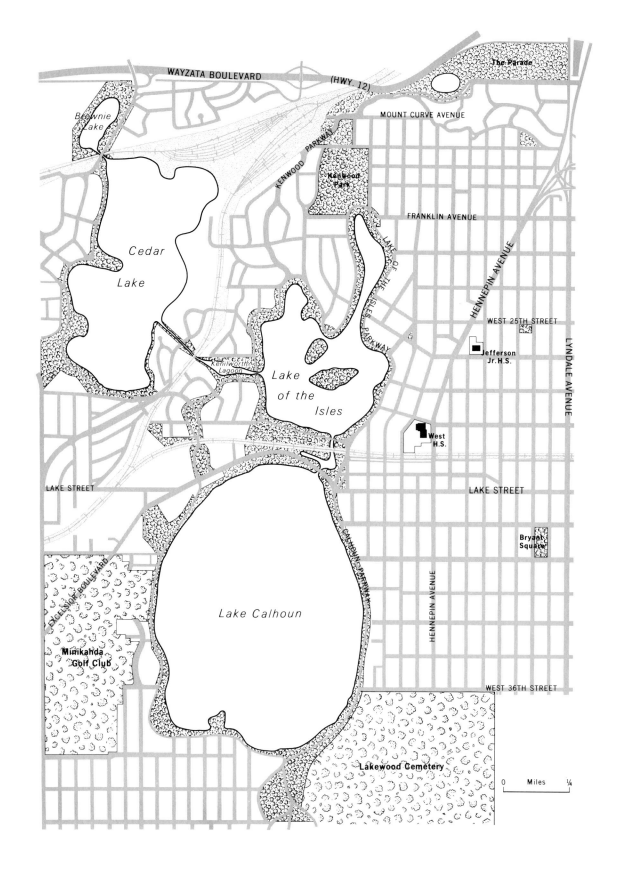

Prologue

To the discerning eye, a landscape can be deciphered and read like a good book or map. We are surrounded by the story of our past, and the face of the land is our most important historical document. Every thread of a place's fabric, no matter how ordinary, has a story to tell — each clump of trees, unusual slope, building or pathway provides visual clues to the sequence of change that gives character to a place. In a location as attractive and exciting as the part of Minneapolis dominated by Lowry Hill, Lake of the Isles and Lake Calhoun, the landscape sings. Here, generations of human occupants have augmented nature to produce one of the most delightful urban settings in North America.

Throughout its colorful history, the lake district, with its several distinctive neighborhoods, has attracted an unique mix of Minneapolis residents. Some came to make their fortune, others to live a splendid life in the manner of a country squire. Some came to establish comfortable family homes, while others to promenade or to revel in the most current fad in outdoor recreation. No matter the year or the season, the lake district has been center stage in Minneapolis.

The influence of Lowry Hill and the lakes extends for several blocks toward the east until the concentration of business and flow of traffic on Lyndale Avenue mark the beginning of a new residential district. On the north and west, the belt of railroad tracks effectively hems in the area. The western edge is less definite. However, the city limits provide a recognizable boundary for most residents. The southern edge has been set at Lakewood Cemetery and the development known in former years as Cottage City because the neighborhoods in the vicinity of Lake Harriet have their own special sense of place.

The landscape surrounding us has been built in phases on the foundation of nature. Each generation has left its mark, either by adding features or destroying older elements. Layer upon layer, the landscape develops until a dramatic change in economics or technology causes a drastic alteration. When one carefully observes, it is frequently possible to see a relic of former times — an extra wide alley marks the route of a long abandoned railroad, an unusual roofline tells us a mansion has been divided into apartments, a solitary oak tree marks the groves of the frontier. All these and other features of the landscape tell us where we are, both in time and space. They illustrate the lifestyles of the former occupants of our neighborhoods and indicate further changes.

But the natural environment provides the foundation of our cities. The lake district is built upon one of the

1

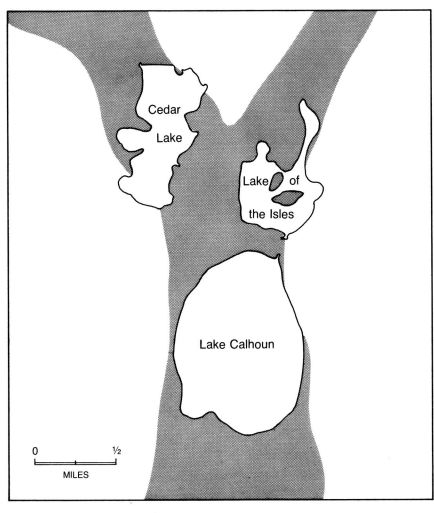

Rivers of water from melting glaciers carved deep valleys below the surface of the lake district. The neighborhood's lakes and low areas are surface expressions of these ancient buried valleys.

most exceptional sets of natural features in the area. Although these hills, valleys and lakes have been changed, they have always been cherished by residents and visitors alike. Although countless fads and fashions have swept through Minneapolis, the lakes have remained the symbol of the best the city has to offer. Before we can comprehend the people of the city, we must understand the lakes.

The Geology of the Lake District

Hundreds of feet below the present surface of the land lie ancient river valleys carved through the bedrock by torrential rivers of meltwater. The meltwater flowed from the face of great glaciers that some 10,000 to 12,000 years ago stood several miles to the north of the present Twin Cities.

During the ice age, the glaciers periodically advanced over the present Minneapolis and Saint Paul. When they melted back they left, in addition to sand and gravel deposits, large blocks of ice — essentially icebergs — stranded in the deep valleys. These blocks of ice were soon covered with windblown dirt. Because of this insulation and the great thickness of the icebergs, the blocks melted more slowly than the rest of the ice. The portion of the valley not occupied by ice was filled in with rock and sand washed down from the surrounding low hills. When the ice blocks eventually melted, they left the shallow lake basins of Cedar, Lake of the Isles, Calhoun, Harriet, and others.

A seal of nearly impermeable clay and very fine particles of sand was formed in the bottom of these depressions as the ice melted. Gradually water from melting snow and summer rains filled the lake beds. With the retreat of the glacier, vegetation advanced into the area. Reeds, grasses and sedges grew on the marshy shores of the lakes. Some plants, animals and fish invaded the lakes and thrived there. Dead vegetation sank to the bottom of the lakes and was covered by silt. Over the years alternating layers of organic and fine mineral particles built up the bottom of the lake and extended the marshy shore out into the lake basin. As a result, rather extensive bogs surrounded the lakes, except where there were low hills. All lakes are temporary features and the process of erosion would have gradually transformed these lakes into marshes, bogs and, eventually, a lowland area.

Like the lakes, the hills of this area are products of glaciation. When the ice sheets stopped advancing, rock material was dropped at the edges in great piles of unsorted rocks, sand and boulders, known as moraines. The Twin Cities are surrounded on the west, south and east by a broad zone of moraines and small lakes, but only a few moraines are found within the city of Minneapolis. Although Lowry Hill is the largest and most famous of these moraines, the hills on both the west and east sides of Lake Calhoun are as high. West of the lake district lies a wide and complex zone of moraines, small lakes and extensive marshes. Most of the southwestern suburbs were swamps when white settlement began. The great marsh to the south of Lake Calhoun nearly reaches the valley of Minnehaha Creek. Tamarack trees from this marsh pro-duced logs for the cabin of the Pond brothers, the first white settlers on Lake Calhoun.

The moraines and outwash plain supported a mixed hardwood forest of sugar maple, basswood, ash, elm, butternut, and oak trees. The forest floor was covered with maple saplings, dogwood, hophorn beam or ironwood, and the variety of flowers included bellwort, anemones, Dutchman's-breeches, bloodroot, trillium, and lady's-slippers. There were also patches of long-grass prairie comprised of bluestem and gamma grass, and annual flowers such as the aster and cone-flower.

This verdant and fertile landscape underwent constant change for thousands of years. New types of grasses and trees replaced those more adapted to the climate at the fringe of glaciers. Fires, started by lightning, raged through the area and set in motion complex sequential changes in the vegetation and animal population. But compared to the alterations that were to occur in the lake district during the last half of the nineteenth century, these changes appear inconsequential.

Cedar Lake's marshy western shore in 1887 resembled a wilderness landscape (Minneapolis Public Library).

CHAPTER 1

Early History

The lake district's swampy shores and grassy forest clearings provided an excellent range for a wide variety of animals and birds. Early accounts indicate that Indians hunted there, but no village was established in the district until 1828.

The Medawakantanwan, one of five major divisions of Dakota-speaking people, controlled the territory. They lived along the Minnesota and Mississippi rivers in villages known as Kaposia, Black Dog's, Chaska's, Shakopee's; maintaining themselves by growing corn and vegetables, as well as hunting and fishing.

By the time American settlers arrived along the upper Mississippi River in the early 1800s, over a century of fur trade had accustomed the native population to European manufactured goods, as well as the customs and behavior of the whites.

To the eager and conscientious first American ambassador to the Indians, Major Lawrence Taliaferro, the idea of converting Indians to farm life seemed not only laudable but practical. Based at Fort Snelling, Taliaferro was appointed Indian agent in 1819, a time when many Indian groups were becoming dependent upon the economy of the fur trade and were moving their settlements to locations near trading posts or forts. Taliaferro believed that the days of hunting and tribal war were doomed, and wished to help establish a new economic system among the Indians based on European agricultural techniques. In 1828 he sponsored a village, which he called Eatonville in honor of John H. Eaton, secretary of war, but known to the Indians as Kay-h yah-ta Otanwa (village whose houses have roofs).

Cloudman's Village

This endeavor was made possible by Cloudman. A Dakota from one of the Minnesota valley villages, Cloudman was an exceptional individual. Not only was he a pacifist, but he also advocated the idea that Indians should live in farming villages. He was scorned by many of his people who wished to guard their traditional customs. Cloudman apparently had become converted to agriculture while snowbound and near death on a western hunting trip. Believing that agriculture might help his people escape such privations, he consulted with Taliaferro about ways to begin a farming community. With the major's support he gathered a few families and established Eatonville on the southeast shore of Lake Calhoun. This area was on the fringe of Dakota territory and could be reached easily from Fort Snelling.

Taliaferro furnished the would-be farmers with seeds, hoes and plows, and hired government farmers to help

Cloudman's Village, the first settlement in the lake district, painted by George Catlin, the noted American artist in 1835 or 1836. (Smithsonian Institution, Washington, D.C.).

them clear the land and plant. Philander Prescott was the first government farmer at Eatonville. According to Prescott's recollections, the early settlement consisted of Cloudman, Prescott's Indian wife, children and father-in-law. "We plowed about a month, but there were few Indians that would venture out that year, as they were afraid of the Chippewas," he wrote.

> We did not do much the first year; still we raised some corn. The Indian agent . . . furnished us with some provisions once in a while and with my gun and fish line we made out to live.

Despite its slow start, by 1830 there were more applicants for a place in Eatonville than could be accommodated. Eighty acres were under plow. The Indians harvested a bumper crop and it appeared that Taliaferro's experiment might be successful after all. Even the men had begun to help with the farm work, duties normally delegated to the women.

The Pond Brothers

In 1831, Taliaferro recognized Cloudman's authority and appointed him chief of the Lake Calhoun tribe. In that year the band truly prospered. About 300 people lived in the village during the growing season, many returning for the winter to their villages along the Minnesota and Mississippi rivers. They raised enough corn and potatoes to enter into trade with Indians living in other villages and with European traders.

In 1834 two lay missionaries, Gideon and Samuel Pond, arrived at Fort Snelling seeking an opportunity to evangelize the Indians. These tall, young men, originally from Connecticut, had been converted at a New England revival meeting in 1831. Samuel had heard of the Minnesota territory and its Dakota population while in Galena, Illinois, searching for a suitable location for their mission work. The Ponds apparently had great faith in their mission. They arrived at Fort Snelling without ordination and lacked a permit for entry into Indian country. They had had no experience as missionaries and practically no knowledge of the Indian language. However, the Ponds were bright, hard-working and enthusiastic. Taliaferro recognized those qualities and helped the men settle with Cloudman's people where they worked as government farmers.

The Pond brothers were primarily interested in converting the population to Christianity. Since knowledge of Dakota was indispensable to a proclamation of the gospel, the Ponds, during their first year in Eatonville, began to study this Indian language by accompanying the Indians on hunting trips. Later, they adapted the English alphabet to Dakota and produced grammar books and even a newspaper in the Dakota language.

But before the Ponds could begin their missionary work, they first had to solve a practical problem — finding a place to live. Cloudman himself selected the site for their cabin on the hill above the eastern shore of Calhoun because from there they could see the loons on the lake.

This cabin, the first European-built structure in the lake district, had two rooms. It measured twelve by sixteen feet and had an eight-foot ceiling and a cellar. The Ponds wrote:

> Straight poles from the tamarack groves west of Lake Calhoun formed the timbers of the roof. The roof itself was bark of trees which grew on the bank of a neighboring creek, fastened with strings of the inner bark of the basswood. Split logs furnished material for the floor; the ceiling was of slabs from the old government mill at Saint Anthony Falls. . . . The Indian Village was on the lower ground south down from the lake toward Lake Harriet.

In a letter to Herman Hine, written in January 1835, Samuel Pond described the sights on a trip from Fort Snelling to the cabin:

> As you draw near the hill first mentioned following an Indian footpath you would see white cloths fixed to the tops of poles. They are waving over graves. The top of the hill is the Indians burying ground who always bury their dead in high places. If you should go to the top of the hill, you would see the hair of surviving

Lawrence Taliaferro, agent and friend of the Indians, founded Eatonville (Cloudman's Village) (T. Gettys, Minnesota Historical Society).

friends which they have cut off and strewed about the graves. They often cut themselves very bad with knives when their friends die. Perhaps too you would see some food which they have laid by the graves for the dead to eat. After passing a little to the right of the burying ground you would turn to [the] left and pass through the corn fields in your way to the village; here you would see the women and girls dressed in something like a petticoat and short gown taking care of their corn. If the corn was ripe enough to eat the men and boys would be there too; if not some of the men and boys would be after deer and some of them would be doing nothing.

Demise of the Indian Village

Although the people of the Lake Calhoun village made great strides in agriculture, the growing population of the band produced rivalries or encouraged existing jealousies among the leadership. However, it was competition among the missionaries that marked the beginning of Eatonville's demise. In the summer of 1835 two fully certified missionaries arrived at Fort Snelling. One, the Reverend Jedediah D. Stevens, established himself on the northwest shore of Lake Harriet. He encouraged the Ponds to help him in building a mission school for Indians. In 1836 they abandoned their house on Lake Calhoun and worked with Stevens. Later that year Gideon Pond moved further west.

In 1837, Stevens and Samuel Pond had a falling out. Stevens did not approve of lay people preaching and expected Pond to do manual labor and act as his interpreter. Pond wrote: "But I did not come here to interpret for anyone — certainly not for one with as little ability natural or acquired as Mr. Stevens, so I determined to go to Connecticut and obtain a license to preach." Upon Pond's return in 1839, Taliaferro appointed him farmer to the Calhoun band. Stevens, realizing the competition was too much for him, left the area.

The year 1839 was to be cataclysmic for the Calhoun band. In April 1838, an Ojibwe named Hole-in-Day killed thirteen Dakota at Lac Qui Parle. Hole-in-Day came to Fort Snelling in July, and two members of the Calhoun band attempted to ambush him. They failed and killed only his companion. In retaliation, Cloudman's son-in-law was killed near Lake Harriet by members of Hole-in-Day's tribe. These killings caused the Dakota-Ojibwe feud to flare into war. Several bloody battles occurred along the Saint Croix and Rum rivers — ninety-five Ojibwe and seventeen Dakota were killed. For a month following their triumph, the Dakota celebrated at Lake Calhoun with scalp dances. During the war, the Ponds' cabin was dismantled and used to fortify Cloudman's village.

The village was on the Dakota-Ojibwe frontier and, consequently, vulnerable to attack. Some warriors from the Lake Calhoun band were killed; the survivors decided to abandon Eatonville and rejoin the villages along the Minnesota River to await better times.

Better times did not come, however. Major Joseph Plympton, commander of Fort Snelling, was named acting agent after Taliaferro resigned around 1839. Plympton refused to allow Indian settlements on the military reservation; the Dakota were, therefore, not allowed to return to Eatonville. When the Treaty of Traverse des Sioux was signed and all the Indian land west of the Mississippi was opened to white settlement, Cloudman and his people were relocated to reservations on the upper Minnesota River.

Major Joseph Plympton's Survey

In the late autumn of 1839, Plympton ordered a survey of the military reserve that was to set in motion the settlement pattern of the lake district.

Thirty-four years earlier, Lieutenant Zebulon Pike had come to Minnesota to purchase a site for a fort that would enable the Americans to control the fur trade. He purchased land at the confluence of the Mississippi and Minnesota rivers for sixty gallons of liquor, $2000 cash and a promise of $2000 to be paid at some future time. Only a small part of that land would be needed for a fortress but military planners wanted to control the approaches to the fort and have enough land to provide a ready supply of firewood and building timber for the fort. In addition, some land was needed for crops. Pike drove a hard bargain, and the army got control of the falls of Saint Anthony, most of what is now south Minneapolis, and a large section of Saint Paul. Until 1835 all the rest of the

Gideon H. Pond (Minnesota Historical Society).

An artist's conception of the Pond brothers' cabin on the east shore of Lake Calhoun (The Bromley Collection, Minneapolis Public Library).

Samuel Pond (Minnesota Historical Society).

land in the territory belonged to the Indians, and the whites could not lay legal claim to it. As a result, most Americans coming to the area to trade were squatters on the military reserve. Many Indians also lived on the reserve to be close to the agent and the traders.

The early commanders of the fort, concerned about construction and defense, paid little attention to the exact limits of their jurisdiction. Once the process of removing Indian title to the land began, however, it became necessary to survey the army's territory. The inter-tribal hostilities of the late 1830s may have influenced the decision to survey the fort, as well.

The survey of Fort Snelling illustrates the major physical and cultural features of the lake district as they were viewed in that unsettled time between the removal of the Indians and the development of the city. The alignment

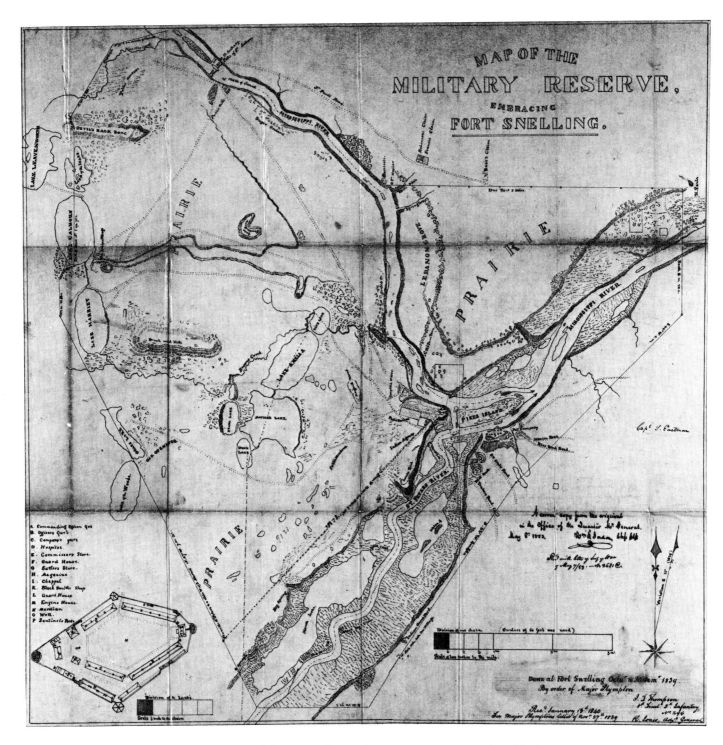

An 1839 map of the Fort Snelling Military Reservation (National Archives).

of the major river courses and lake basins is correct, although the map maker seems to have underestimated the size of Lake Calhoun and Lake Harriet. Looking first at the east side of Lake Calhoun, we see the site of the abandoned Eatonville, labelled "old Indian Village." We know the village was abandoned when this map was made because occupied sites are indicated by the name of the local chief, such as Black Dog's village on the Minnesota (then called Saint Peter's) River.

Almost all of what we now call south Minneapolis was a prairie when this map was made. To the south of the lake district were several areas of mixed prairie and oak groves known as oak openings, and further east on the banks of the Mississippi gorge was a large stand of sugar maple trees that were regularly tapped by the military for maple syrup. A few of the place names have been changed. Cedar Lake was then called Leavenworth in honor of the first commander of the fort, and the large moraine known today as Lowry Hill had been given the lurid title of "the Devil's Back Bone."

As might be expected, Eatonville was connected by major trails both to the mills located near Saint Anthony Falls and to the Indian agency and fort. The road from the village to what is now downtown Minneapolis follows almost a straight-line route and at no time coincides with the route of modern Hennepin Avenue. Both trails to the east parallelled a sizable ravine, which lies between modern Thirty-sixth and Thirty-eighth avenues south, passing well south of the marshy Powderhorn Lake. Clearly the soldiers at the fort were greatly impressed by the two hills near the lakes, but they had not named the heavily wooded hill located to the southeast of Lake Harriet, now called Washburn Park.

The logic behind Taliaferro's selection of the shores of Lake Calhoun for his experiment with Indian agriculture is quite apparent from this map. The site was one of the few that was far enough away from the fort to satisfy security needs yet still within the reserve. In addition, it was in a well-watered but adequately drained area on the edge of a large open prairie. Consequently, the farmers would not have to fell large numbers of trees before they could begin plowing. We can also see why the Pond brothers had to bring logs for their cabin from the

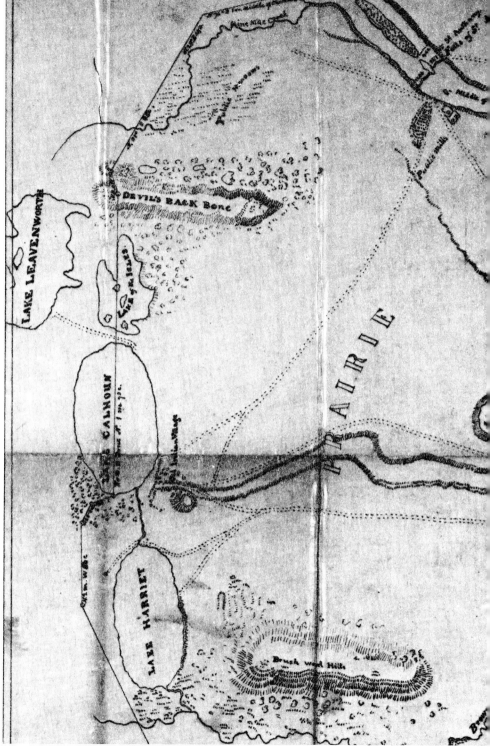

Key features of the lake district are visible on this enlargement of the 1839 map.

The lake district as depicted in the 1874 Andreas Atlas.

tamarack grove on the other side of the lake; there was simply no timber in the vicinity.

The Minneapolis land rush that began in 1845 when the west bank of the Mississippi was first cleared of Indian title did not have an immediate impact on the lake district. Early settlers were much more interested in the land close to the bridge and Saint Anthony Falls sites than in the marshy shores of the lakes. Those lands went unclaimed until the winter of 1849 when Charles Mosseaux, a French Canadien voyageur employed by the American Fur Company, received permission from the commander of Fort Snelling to stake out a claim on the east side of Lake Calhoun. Mosseaux proceeded to build a shanty on the site of Pond's cabin and mission, and one assumes he cultivated the old Indian fields. He occupied the claim until moving to Minneapolis in 1857 to work as a carpenter and painter. He sold his land in 1879 to William S. King and it was incorporated into the Lyndale Farm. John Berry was the first farmer near Lake of the Isles.

The First Minneapolis Land Boom

In 1853 the military reserve was thrown open to civilian settlement, and Minneapolis was founded. In 1854 a bridge was built crossing the Mississippi upstream from Saint Anthony Falls. The square at its western terminus became the focus for the city, with the first businesses located on Hennepin Avenue at Bridge Square. The bridge forced a reorientation of all the major roads on the west bank, and the first blocks platted in the city were aligned with the river's edge. These river-oriented blocks extend from roughly Plymouth Avenue on the north to Cedar on the south. Later, as the city expanded, the river frontage became less important and developments were laid out according to the cardinal directions. This adjustment of the grid of streets confuses residents and newcomers alike. It is also the cause of the Hennepin-Lyndale bottleneck, one of the district's most notorious landmarks.

The year 1857 produced the first land boom in Minneapolis. Population increased from about 200 to 2000 people in two years, and real estate development was booming. Nearly everyone speculated in land. The

Boating on Lake Calhoun
was a popular pastime
in the late nineteenth century
(Minnesota Historical Society).

wealthy platted entire blocks, while the less well-off bought one or two city lots and waited for the tide of immigration to make them wealthy. Despite their dreams of dramatic expansion, settlement crowded close to the Saint Anthony Falls and bridge sites throughout the Civil War era. Rail service reached the city from Saint Paul in 1867 and by 1869 a thriving commercial district developed along lower Hennepin Avenue. By this time a series of annexations in 1856, 1866 and 1867 had pushed the western city limits as far as Lowry Hill.

Farmers and speculators purchased all the land in the lake district during the years before the Civil War. Developers opened the northern and eastern sections of the district for middle class residents during the late 1860s but, as the map of Minneapolis in 1874 indicates, most of the land in the area was divided into large parcels owned by farmers and speculators.

Many of the city's most famous early settlers engaged in land speculation in the district. John Green farmed land near the hill formerly called the Devil's Backbone.

Colonel William S. King (Minnesota Historical Society).

The large parcel to the west of Green's was owned by J. C. Goodrich who was apparently a speculator. Thomas Lowry, founder of the Twin Cities' streetcar system, owned land directly on the Devil's Backbone — later to be known as Lowry Hill — along with his father-in-law C. G. Goodrich. Goodrich was a prominent physician who became wealthy through his investments in real estate. He was involved in many public enterprises and was the first president of the Lakewood Cemetery Association.

The land fronting on Hennepin Avenue was divided into small parcels but the large block fronting on the east side of Lake of the Isles was owned by C. G. Goodrich in partnership with others. Thomas Halloran lived on his land between Lake of the Isles and Cedar Lake, but he had no close neighbors. The southeastern shore of Lake of the Isles was owned by R. P. Russell, a New Englander who came west to seek his fortune in 1839. An active merchant and politician, he dabbled in many financial matters including lumber, milling, land development, and farming.

The primary path of development in the city during this period was in the vicinity of the Washburns' estates, south of Franklin and west of Portland. This growth pattern influenced other developers to plat "outlots" or suburban tracts beyond the city limits. Most of the area on Lyndale between Franklin and Lake was divided into lots at this time, and one development was established between Hennepin and Lyndale just north of Lake. However, this subdivision was well beyond the zone of active residential building.

William S. King's Lyndale Farm

Most of the land in the district was owned by Colonel William S. King. King was a truly extraordinary man who influenced the city and neighborhood in several ways. His Lyndale Farm was the largest solely-owned property in the history of Minneapolis. King hoped to live the life of a country squire on his magnificent country estate that stretched from Thirty-fourth Street south to Lake Harriet, between Lyndale and Hennepin Avenue.

King was active in all sorts of endeavors but his pri-

The Lyndale farmstead was built in 1870 near 35th Street and Bryant Avenue (Minneapolis Park and Recreation Board).

mary occupations were journalist, publisher and politician. He founded the **State Atlas**, a radical republican newspaper that was merged into the **Minneapolis Tribune** in 1867. Always active in political causes, he was elected to Congress and spoke on a variety of issues from the abolition of slavery to governmental subsidies. He was instrumental in the establishment of the Minnesota State Fair and participated in the organization of the Lakewood Cemetery Association.

In the early 1870s, King felt a twinge of nostalgia for the farm life he had led as a child. He began acquiring the land that lay around the lakes, purchasing the Deacon Mann pre-emption at Lake Harriet, the Father Gear claim at Lake Calhoun, and the Manwaring tract near Harriet, among others. He soon owned 1400 acres.

The Lyndale Farm held spacious barns and a large farmhouse. King gathered choice English breeds of cattle, including the shorthorn, Ayrshire and Jersey. He held annual sales; at one it is reported that a Bates bull brought $14,000. Although King lived in his fine house until his death, his estate was the subject of litigation, eventually being subdivided for building lots in the 1880s.

The Resort Era

By the 1870s the lakes were attracting all sorts of people seeking relief from the congestion and dirt of the

Sailboats on Lake Calhoun in the early 1880s. Note the simple hotel and boat rental facility on the northeast shore (Jacoby, Minnesota Historical Society).

The Lyndale, an elegant resort hotel located on the east shore of Lake Calhoun during the booming 1880s (Minnesota Historical Society).

central city. Although Henry David Thoreau was enthusiastic about the wildlife along the shore of the lakes, most people who visited the area came to fish or enjoy the cool breezes and fresh air. These tourists wanted comfort and several people were delighted to provide it for them.

Louis Menage developed a resort hotel on the western shore of Lake Calhoun, where the Minikahda Club now stands. This 130-acre tract was known as Menage's Lake Side Park and the hotel was called the Lake Side Park Hotel. People came to the park for picnics, as well as longer visits, and delighted in the eighty foot high wooden observatory built on the hill. Visitors came to the site across the lake on a small steamer. The Lake Side had to contend with competition from the Calhoun House, which was built on the north side of the lake in 1879, and the Lake Calhoun Pavilion, built on the site of the Pond cabin by King in 1877. Constructed upon the hill above the eastern shore, the Pavilion had verandas on its third and fourth floors that provided a view of sunsets and the surrounding countryside. The weekly parties held there were an important part of the city's social life.

The Pavilion was taken over and extensively remodeled just after mid-summer in 1883 by Louis Menage. Renamed "the Lyndale," the new hotel was heralded as the city's "long needed first class hotel." It was expected that the Lyndale would put Minneapolis on an even footing with Saint Paul. Located close to the station of the Minneapolis, Lyndale and Lake Minnetonka Railway, the Lyndale was only twenty minutes from downtown. It was, of course, elegantly furnished and

lighted by gas manufactured on the premises: has hot and cold water and electric bells in all the rooms, steam heating apparatus in all the halls and bathrooms, and its baths and closets are filled with the most approved appliances made.

Naturally, a hotel of this importance had to have a gala opening. The event, presented by a committee that included Lowry and King, was a dinner dance for 150 couples. The "beauty and chivalry" of the Twin Cities were there, and they danced and dined the night away. When the party ended near dawn the following day, Colonel William McCrory placed a special train at the guests' disposal. It was, they said, "the social event of the season."

The excitement did not last long, however. The Lyndale soon went the way of so many large wooden structures in the nineteenth century, being destroyed by fire around 1888. This fire brought the resort era on Lake Calhoun to an end.

"A CHARMING RETREAT."

The Oak Grove House, a resort hotel on Cedar Lake, was extolled by its guests as having the purest air in the state (Minnesota Historical Society).

The trains of the main line of the St. Paul & Pacific R. R. leave for the "Home," distant five minutes by boat or carriage (*free of charge*) from Cedar Lake Station, fifteen miles from St. Paul, and only three-and-one-half miles from Minneapolis, as follows:

GOING, LEAVE ST. PAUL, 7:55 A. M. and 3:40 P. M.
"   "   MINNEAPOLIS, 8:40 A. M. and 4:35 P. M.
RETURNING, LEAVE THE "HOME" AT 8:30 A. M. and 6:50 P. M.

All places of interest can be visited by railroad, or carriages kept for that purpose, at reasonable prices, after rest from travel. *Check through*, and if not suited it will cost nothing to leave.

TERMS : For single rooms, $ 3.00 per day.
"   "   "   14.00 " week.
"   "   "   50.00 " month.

The use of boats included, a discount from the latter price for the season.

From the St. Paul and Minneapolis Papers.

17

Mass transportation between the lake district and the city was first provided by McCrory's "Minneapolis, Lyndale and Lake Calhoun" street railway. McCrory also owned the "Hattie" (Minnesota Historical Society).

CHAPTER 2

Streetcars & Parks

Boom town! Even the most ardent city boosters of the 1870s could not predict the explosion of wealth and population that Minneapolis was to enjoy during the fifteen years between 1880 and 1895. The city's population had increased threefold during the 1870s, going from slightly over 18,000 to almost 47,000. But by 1885 the population had grown to 129,000, and in 1890 it reached 164,738. The state census of 1895 counted 192,833. In a quarter century the population had increased eleven times over and a city was built. Nearly everyone speculated in real estate. Land prices skyrocketed and astute investors amassed fortunes overnight.

The periodic financial panics that swept the country took the edge off the boom, but the economy was fundamentally sound. The rapid development of the city in this period was a direct response to establishment of new forms of economic activity and discovery of new resources in the rural areas served by Minneapolis.

The two basic industries of Minneapolis both reached their peak shortly after the turn of the century. Lumbering, milling and woodworking plants actually peaked in 1899 and were essentially gone from the city by 1919. Flour milling reached its peak in 1915, but its importance diminished more slowly. As a result, the growth rate for Minneapolis leveled off; the population increased to 180,000 by 1920.

The handful of stores, offices and houses that clustered at Bridge Square on lower Hennepin Avenue attracted most of the early settlers. By 1875, in fact, 49 percent of the city's population lived within a mile of the city center, crowding together to live close to the places at which they worked, shopped and socialized. In a time when nearly everyone walked, commuting distances had to be kept to a minimum. The congestion of the early city was not pleasant and most everyone wished to escape the noise, dirt and odors of a city that contained more horses and cows than people. Those families that could afford to maintain horses, the wealthy, were seeking out residences on the edge of the city in areas that had some natural beauty such as hills or water. The lake district was the result of their search for convenience and beauty.

Mass Transportation and the Expansion of the City

Real estate developers realized that if they could devise a cheap form of transportation, one that would enable the middle class worker to commute longer distances, they would be able to sell vast acreage for suburban development. They all knew what was needed — a street railroad, a machine that could carry large numbers of people at low cost. Their problem was twofold: money and technology. Cities in Europe and on the eastern seaboard had experimented with oversize carriages called omnibuses pulled by horses and using the city streets. They were top heavy, however, and had an unfortunate tendency to tip over on the muddy and uneven streets of frontier settlements. Other inventors had developed horse drawn railroads that, while more expensive to construct, were more reliable.

In the 1860s, several individuals petitioned the city council for the exclusive franchise to operate a street railroad in Minneapolis. A franchise was granted, but no building began until the early 1870s. At that time George Washburn, Colonel William S. King and others attempted to build a system that would connect the milling district with the residential districts in south Minneapolis. Their venture failed.

Finally, a businessman emerged who was capable of developing and managing a successful and extensive streetcar system. Thomas Lowry, a lawyer from Illinois, came to Minneapolis in 1867 to seek his fortune. Child of a pioneer family, he had experienced land booms in his youth, apparently realized what was going to happen in the new city, and began to acquire suburban land. The demand for real estate dropped dramatically during the panic of 1873. As a result Lowry began to search for a way to increase the marketability of his property. Like others, his attention was attracted to the potentials of the horsecar.

In 1875 at the ripe old age of thirty-two, Lowry, together with King, reorganized the original Min-

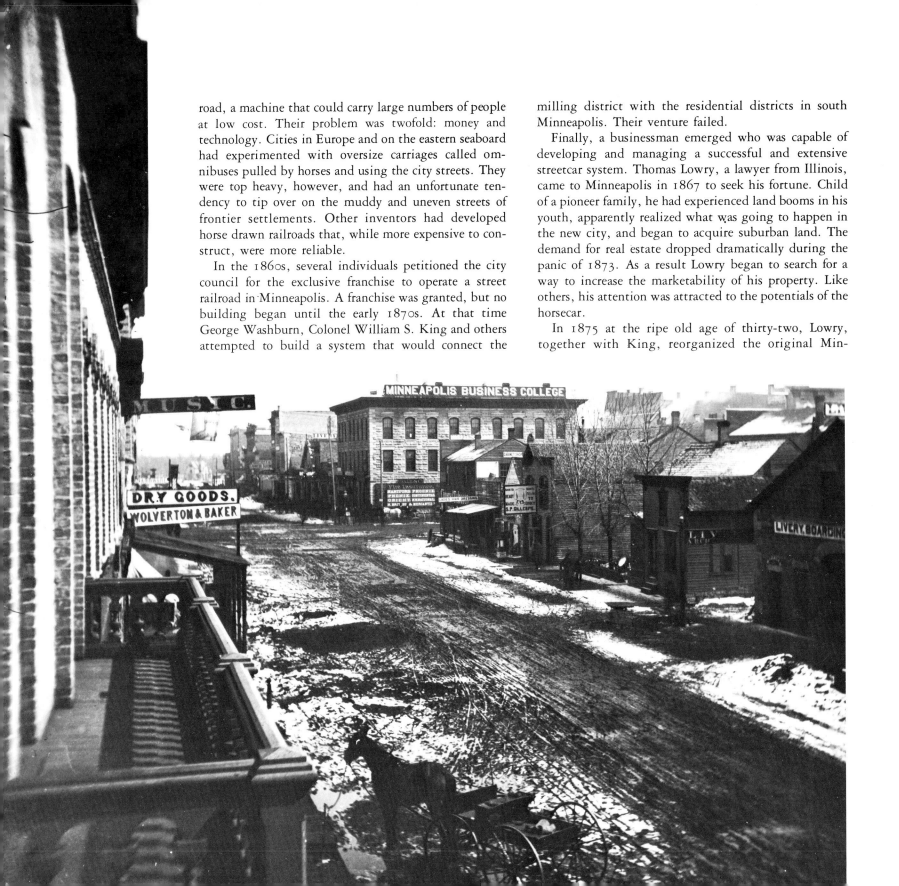

Left, Nicollet Avenue in 1874 (Bromley Collection, Minneapolis Public Library).
Above and right, Thomas Lowry and his wife, Beatrice. Thomas Lowry came
to Minneapolis in 1867, determined to make his fortune in the booming town.
Beatrice was a daughter of C. G. Goodrich (Minnesota Historical Society).

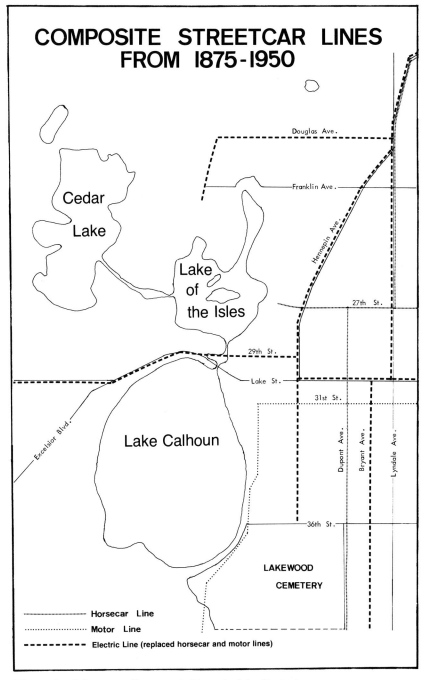

COMPOSITE STREETCAR LINES FROM 1875-1950

Cedar Lake

Lake of the Isles

Lake Calhoun

Douglas Ave.

Franklin Ave.

Hennepin Ave.

27th St.

29th St.

Lake St.

31st St.

36th St.

Excelsior Blvd.

Dupont Ave.

Bryant Ave.

Lyndale Ave.

LAKEWOOD CEMETERY

·············· Horsecar Line

·············· Motor Line

- - - - - - Electric Line (replaced horsecar and motor lines)

The tracks of the street railway reached into the lake district in several stages. At first horsecars connected the northern section to downtown. Later the entire district was linked to the rest of the city by rapid transit.

neapolis Street Railway Company, using the money of Philo Osgood, an investor from Ilion, New York. Their first line ran on both sides of the river from the campus of the University of Minnesota to Washington and Fourth streets in downtown. At first the line was not particularly profitable. The city's franchise limited the fare to five cents, and the company's expenses were high. It was necessary to lay a roadbed and track through the city's unpaved streets at a cost of $6000 per mile. Operational costs were also a problem. For example, six horses costing between $135 and $150 apiece, were needed for each car. In 1875, receipts averaged $37 a day. They rose to $55 per day in 1876 and $85 in 1877. Workers did not receive their wages on time, and the company was constantly hounded by creditors.

Lowry continued to invest actively in real estate, but he was also convinced that the streetcar franchise would be one of the most valuable franchises in the country. He took over the controlling interest in 1877. He was steadfast in his belief that lines should be constructed in advance of the population movement, even though he was forced personally to guarantee the heavy load of debt this policy forced upon the company.

The company was known to be losing money, yet developers made constant demands for the extension of existing lines and the building of new tracks into their properties. The proximity of horsecar tracks increased the demand for house lots and caused a great differential in land values. Everyone appeared to believe that the horsecar line should be operated, even at a loss, just as long as they would be able to maximize profit on the land through which it ran.

In 1890, when the horsecar system was reasonably well established with 218 cars, 1018 horses and 66.67 miles of track, the demand for modernization forced the company to convert — first to cable cars and then to streetcars. Installation of cable cars in other cities prompted the Minneapolis Street Railway in 1890 to buy cable equipment and material worth $300,000. Most of this was never used because in the course of the next year Minneapolis, like other cities across North America, began to electrify the system.

In order to make the conversion, Lowry had to return

to the capital markets of the East. There he got the financial backing he needed, but he was forced to unite the Saint Paul Street Railway system with the Minneapolis company. This was not a difficult merger because Lowry already controlled both companies. Electrification was completed in 1892 just in time for the financial panic of 1893 and for severe competition from the latest fad in urban transportation, the bicycle. Bicycling was so popular between 1893 and 1896 that it cut into the earnings of the company.

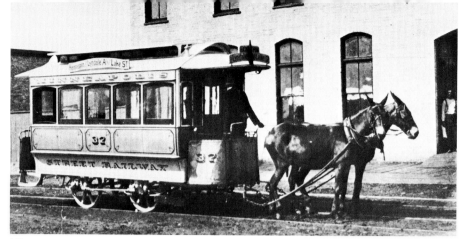

The new Hennepin-Lyndale horsecar in 1876 (Minneapolis Public Library).

The Impact of the Streetcar Lines

Contractors and real estate promoters reacted enthusiastically to the building of horsecar lines in the lake district. Their first projects were concentrated in the East Lowry Hill and Carag neighborhoods, that is, in the Wedge between Hennepin, Lyndale and Thirty-sixth streets. This area was attractive to residential developers because it was served by one of the city's first horsecar lines, which ran from the center of the city along Hennepin Avenue to Lyndale, south on Lyndale to Twenty-seventh Street and west on Twenty-seventh to Dupont. Although there was only limited building along the southern reaches of the line, the northern area was divided into narrow lots. This practice enabled the builders to crowd a large number of units into their area. A typical block in 1892, a decade after the area was platted, might have four to eight houses, many of which were close replicas of each other. For example, in the 2900 block of Aldrich Avenue, three homes next door to each other were all built for Sarah Harrison by May 7, 1886. Each house cost $3000 to build.

The electrification of the carlines hastened the growth of new residential districts. It is interesting to note that the first routes of the carlines ran to Lowry's property in the southern portion of the Groveland Addition and to the northern section of King's property.

By 1903 much of the area between Twenty-sixth and Twenty-eighth on Lyndale and on Hennepin was built up. Small businesses sprang up on Lyndale to serve the streetcar commuters. Shortly after the turn of the cen-

Above, the Bryant Avenue car in a 1930s flood (Minneapolis Public Library).
Below, Thomas Lowry's private streetcar (Minneapolis Public Library).

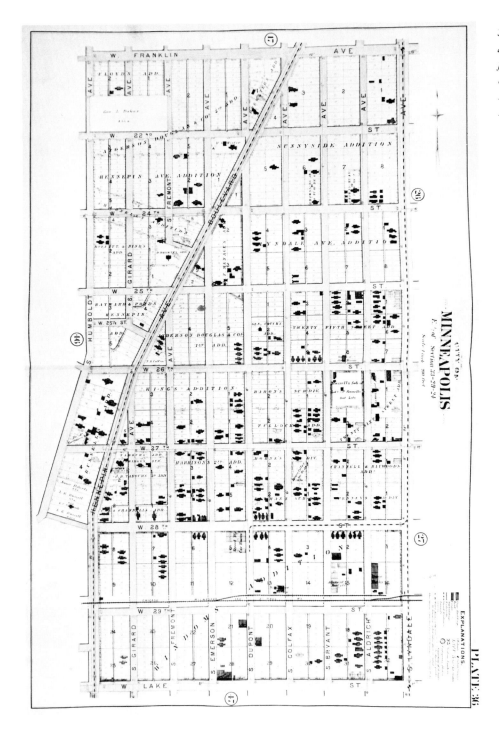

Streetcars made the suburbs attractive for middle class families such as those who built the houses shown on this 1892 map (Minnesota Historical Society).

tury, a thriving business community developed at the corner of Lyndale Avenue and Lake Street.

The area west of Hennepin was also greatly influenced by the Douglas Avenue and Kenwood carline. A few homes were built directly on Douglas but most riders went to the Kenwood Station at the end of the line. There, at the corner of Penn Avenue and Twenty-first Street a tiny cluster of businesses was established. A few shops remain at this same location today.

The Motor Line and Long Distance Commuting

Although streetcars were to become the most important form of mass transit in the lake district, the greatest boost to early development of the area around Lake Calhoun came from the Minneapolis, Lyndale and Lake Calhoun Railway. The company was headed by Colonel William McCrory, a Civil War veteran from Ohio, who received a franchise to operate steam trains on the streets of Minneapolis in 1879. The route left downtown from the intersection of First and Washington, followed Nicollet Avenue to Thirty-first Street where it branched, a single line of tracks going south to Fiftieth in the vicinity of the Washburn Home for Orphans, and the other branch going west on Thirty-first to a station at the Pavilion owned by King. The directors of the Lyndale Railway, or the Motor Line as it was called, hoped to tap the potential market provided by the resort business on Lake Calhoun.

McCrory's railroad ran on a shoestring and started with two used cars and engines that he purchased from eastern railroads. The underpowered motors had trouble with the hill on Nicollet, especially when the tracks were wet. The cars could carry about sixty people in tolerable

The north shore of Lake Calhoun viewed from Lake Street in the late winter of 1902; ice warehouses dominated the shore (Minnesota Historical Society).

style. Trains ran on a forty-five minute schedule from early morning to 10:15 p.m. Because the company had no facilities to turn the trains around, the engines backed out of town. Passengers who wanted a ride simply flagged the train down and, when necessary, waded out to the tracks through the unpaved suburban streets.

In order to increase business, the company operated a small excusion steamer on Lake Calhoun, but the venture was not profitable. The Motor Line was losing money because Lake Calhoun was not becoming the center of pastoral resorts that McCrory and others had expected. Instead, people were attracted to the twelve small hotels built between 1867 and 1879 on the shores of Lake Minnetonka. On the north shore of Minnetonka large, lavish tourist hotels were constructed as well, and estates developed quite rapidly in 1879 and on during the 1880s.

Developments on Calhoun could not keep pace, and, as a result, the Motor Line extended its tracks to Lake Harriet in 1880 and in 1881 to the steamboat docks at Excelsior, on Lake Minnetonka. It then changed its name to the Minneapolis, Lyndale and Minnetonka Railway. Two standard steam locomotives pulled the cars out to

The motor line leaves the Lyndale Hotel c. 1880 (Minnesota Historical Society).

25

Lake Minnetonka, but they were not allowed to run on the city streets. Even though it cost one dollar — a laboring man's daily wage — to ride from Minneapolis to Minnetonka, six daily trains were required to handle the summer traffic. Trains to Lake Calhoun from downtown ran at twenty minute intervals.

Although an army officer during the Civil War, McCrory seems to have been fascinated by ships. After his Calhoun steamer failed, he tried again on Minnetonka. He had an iron-hulled steamboat built and launched, but it could not compete with the established boatlines on the lake and was soon sold. Although business kept expanding, the railroad lost money each winter when people moved back to town and stopped using the lake. Charles Pillsbury took over the company in 1885, but he was not able to boost traffic. The route from Lake Harriet to Lake Minnetonka was abandoned in 1886, and the company was sold to the Minneapolis Street Railway Company in 1887. By 1890 all the routes had been electrified. The entire lake district was served by electric streetcars in 1891.

The Park System

Clearly the presence of the parks and parkways in western Minneapolis make it one of the Twin Cities' most attractive neighborhoods. Residents identify with the recreational landscape, and, for many, life without this attractive public open space would be unthinkable. In the first decades of the city's history, however, the need for parks was one of the most hotly debated topics in the civic arena. Several unsuccessful attempts were made to establish city parks during the 1850s and 1860s. In 1872 King, serving as congressman in Washington, D.C., offered to sell 250 acres around Lake Harriet to the city for $50,000 if it were made into a park. His offer met with a great deal of cynicism. He was informed that he should return to Washington instead of trying to unload his farm on the city for such an inflated price. Finally in 1882 the city council passed a resolution in favor of parks, and several small areas in the central portion of the city were acquired. No lakeshore purchases were made at that time, however.

The city grew at an astounding rate during the early 1880s. The population was swelling with new immigrants, and developers were actively pushing out the limits of the incorporated area. While this growth was enriching real estate speculators and developers it was also alarming many public-spirited individuals who feared that the city would become another industrial slum. They felt that the city needed parks to ease the congestion and provide the population with fresh air and a respite from the monotonous urban landscape.

In response to these feelings, King reorganized a group of private citizens known as the Board of Trade. In 1882 under the leadership of George A. Pillsbury and King, this group began an intensive campaign for city-wide improvements and, especially, a park system. They soon concluded that the city needed a park commission that would be empowered to raise money, as well as establish and maintain a system of parks. They drafted a resolution to that effect for submission to the state legislature.

King believed the city had dallied too long and said

> No subject can be brought up which has such an effect upon the interests of the city. It is a scheme which will bring more capital, more population, and add more to the city's renown than any other scheme which could be devised. Two years ago, we could have bought seven hundred acres of ground around the lake for $50,000 and today the property is worth $300,000.00 but no one would move in the matter and the opportunity was lost. For what is a mere bagatelle now we can lay out a system of parks which will be the pride of the city for all time to come.

The Board of Trade suggested that the park commission be established with an initial appropriation of $100,000, and a public meeting was scheduled on the proposal. The city council was furious. Council members resented the fact that the board was to be totally independent of them, and they were not about to stand by and watch the city's wealthy establish an independent governmental body. But the Board of Trade took the resolution to the state legislature after getting the approval of the Minneapolis delegation. The rules of the legislature were suspended so that a rapid decision could

Decorative hedges and trees mark the edge of East Calhoun Boulevard in 1892 (Minnesota Historical Society).

be made. The bill passed with little difficulty, and the issue was put to a vote of the citizens of Minneapolis.

At this time the Knights of Labor, a nineteenth century version of a trade union, entered into the debate. A meeting of the general membership passed a resolution denouncing the park concept as a cunning scheme by which the rich were to be made richer and the poor poorer.

Despite the opposition of the politicians and Knights of Labor, the measure won an overwhelming vote of approval in the referendum, and the park board was established. In the flush of victory, the board members resolved to congratulate the voters on their wisdom. Their action would make it possible for Minneapolis to join "the very rank of those cities which add to their commercial and financial facilities, the highest possible embellishment of rural beauty."

Cleveland's Park Plan

In April 1883, the new board, under the leadership of Thomas Lowry, hired one of the best landscape architects of the time, H. W. S. Cleveland, to produce a plan of action. By June, Cleveland was ready to report. He advocated boulevards rather than a series of small parks; he felt that small parks had only a local interest while grand ornamental parkways would have city-wide impact. In addition, Cleveland disliked the practice of building decorative structures in the parks. He preferred that the vistas be kept as natural as possible. It was his opinion that once boulevards were laid out and landscaped, fine residences and commercial structures would be built along them. The facades of these structures would provide all the artistic embellishment needed by the city.

A park booster as well as planner, Cleveland urged the board members to have faith in the future greatness of their city. They were to look forward a century to the present era and anticipate the needs for open space. Cleveland dismissed all arguments against parks by pointing out the increase in land value and property taxes associated with the development of New York's Central Park. He considered parks an investment, not a luxury.

Cleveland grasped the significance of the Mississippi River in the development of the city and appreciated the grandeur of the gorge. He made it the focus of his park plan and pleaded with the board to preserve its beauty:

> It is due therefore, to the sentiments of the civilized world and equally in recognition of your own sense of the blessings it confers upon you, that it should be placed in a setting worthy of so priceless a jewel.

27

Cleveland was concerned about the conditions of south Minneapolis. He saw it becoming thickly built-up with houses for middle and lower class families and wanted the board to make a portion of the area so attractive that it would be eagerly sought after. He suggested that they turn Lake Street into a tremendous boulevard 200 feet wide for its entire length from the river west to Lake Calhoun. He said this plan would create a "rich and elegant quarter, in what would otherwise be liable to become a weary and monotonous series of ordinary dwellings and shops." The boulevard would also provide a protection against the spread of fire. Residents in nineteenth century cities lived in constant fear and danger of fires, so this feature of Cleveland's plan was, indeed, attractive. The plan was too expensive, however.

The rest of Cleveland's ideas proved more feasible. A parkway around the lakes would begin at the western terminus of Lake Street and follow the northern, western and southern shores of Lake Calhoun until it reached what is now Thirty-eighth Street. He proposed that the boulevard continue east along Thirty-eighth to Hennepin and then turn north along Hennepin, which was to be a boulevard from that point to its junction with Lyndale. Lyndale was to be made into a boulevard, as well. In addition, he suggested that the entire south shore of Lake Calhoun, then known as the Cottage City Addition, be incorporated into a large park that would join the two lakes. The board had already decided to construct a boulevard around Lake Harriet, and Cleveland supported this plan. The board accepted Cleveland's plan for a system of parks throughout Minneapolis and was successful in carrying out most aspects of the proposal.

Park board negotiations for the purchase of Lake Harriet began in 1883 but the price was too high and the project was abandoned in 1884. Later in that same year the purported landowners involved — James Merritt, Henry Beard and C. McReeve — gave the park board the land, with the provision that they not be assessed for building the boulevard. The offer was accepted, but these men did not have clear title to the land. King, the rightful owner of the property gave this land and an adjacent parcel to the park board in the spring of 1885.

The Parkway System

Hennepin Avenue was designated a parkway in 1884, but no special improvements were made to it until 1886. In the two years between 1886 and 1888 most of the land in the parks of the lake district was acquired. The large section of Calhoun's east shore, most of Lake of the Isles, Dean Boulevard and Kenwood Parkway areas and the islands in the Lake of the Isles were acquired either by direct purchase, condemnation or donation. The board was especially happy to acquire the islands because they were platted for residential use by a developer named Russell. If Russell's plans for this area had come to fruition, the character of the lake would have been entirely different. In the northern part of the district, property owners along what was then Superior Street donated a strip of land 100 feet wide and graded a parkway on it at their own expense. The board accepted their donation and Kenwood Parkway, a central link in the city's boulevard system was developed. In 1890, the area known as Interlachen was purchased for $113,000 and a boulevard connecting lakes Harriet and Calhoun was planned. In addition, the Lakewood Cemetery Association donated thirty-five acres of marshy land on the north shore of Lake Harriet to the city for park use. This was augmented by a tract of equal size lying to the immediate east given by King. In 1892 the last pieces of the present-day lakeside parks were purchased and East Lake of the Isles and East Calhoun Boulevards were connected. The purchase price of these lands was assessed against the adjacent property owners. The acquisition of the area known as the Parade began that same year.

The Hennepin and Lyndale boulevards provided the board a great many problems. Although all recognized that these streets attracted substantial homes, the streets had both been territorial highways and were also important links in the city's transportation system. Following Cleveland's plan in 1884, the park board widened, paved and planted trees along them and attempted to control traffic. Before long, the street became the most fashionable route to the lake. The truckers objected to the traffic restrictions, however, and the park board was taken to court over the issue. The court ruled that the board had

Minneapolis park commissioners in 1914 prepare for a tree planting campaign around Lake Calhoun (Hennepin County Historical Society).

no right to restrict traffic on boulevards that were formerly highways. As a result, the parkways were vacated in 1905. One cannot but help wonder what the district would be like today if Hennepin had remained a residential boulevard.

Transforming the Landscape

Natural and rural beauty did not mean wilderness to the Victorian landscape architects, park enthusiasts and real estate developers. Nature needed to be helped and lakes managed as water landscapes or they would not be attractive. Therefore, in 1892 the board began to transform the marshy shores of the lakes into usable land by dredging and filling.

The rapid progress of the project and the tremendous improvement in the nature of the park produced a building boom in the adjacent neighborhoods and throughout the lake district. A real estate developer, Henry Newhall, believed that the park improvement brought an increase in property values along the lake of between 100 percent and 500 percent, depending on the nature of the lot. According to Theodore Wirth, perhaps the city's most influential superintendent of parks:

> The transformation of those formerly mosquito-infested, malaria-breeding swamplands into clear, deep water areas surrounded by parklands of outstanding beauty naturally had beneficial results upon the city as a whole and was a strong inducement for like operations in other areas offering similar opportunities for improvements.

The success of the dredging operation on Lake of the Isles spurred the board to rework Cedar Lake. During the

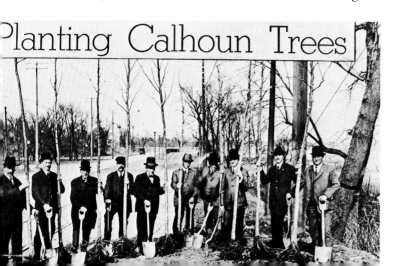

Ladies in the family take a back seat in a 1908 artist's conception of touring in Minneapolis (Minnesota Historical Society).

1870s this lake had also been a popular spot for resort activities. The Oak Grove Hotel stood on the site now occupied by the Jones-Harrison Home for the Elderly. A resort was also established on the eastern shore known as Stetson Cedar Lake Park, attracting an exuberant crowd. In 1908 the board acquired most of the shoreline of the lake and in 1911 dredging operations began. The coarse gravel on the bed of the lake made the operation very difficult and the task was not finished until 1917.

The combination of parks, boulevards, accessible water surfaces and good transportation to downtown and other parts of Minneapolis, made the lake district a real estate developer's dream. The area had everything a promoter could ask. There was no need to exaggerate the district's merits. To sell building lots one only needed to recite the facts. It was the most picturesque neighborhood in the city. It had the most extensive expanses of public open space. It was the home of the city's elite. It did contain good housing for working households; well served by public transportation. Minneapolis was growing and the district was prime real estate. Every speculator in the city knew its value and competition for control of the district was keen. Only the most accomplished operators would be able to develop its neighborhoods.

29

A Minneapolis real estate office in 1857 (Bromley Collection, Minneapolis Public Library).

CHAPTER 3

The Founding of the Neighborhoods

Nineteenth century Minneapolis, like all frontier towns, was filled with adventurers. Perhaps the most aggressive and visionary group of opportunists were the men who attempted to make a living, and even rise to social prominence, through the sale and management of real estate.

The lake district, the most attractive part of Minneapolis, was developed by a handful of investors and promoters, active from 1870 to the late 1890s. These men had grand visions of the future. They had faith in their plans and risked fortunes in a nearly unregulated land market. Naturally they disagreed with each other and on several occasions completely changed their own minds about the potential of an area. As we have seen, Thomas Lowry and Colonel William McCrory were key people in the growth of this part of the city because they established the transportation lines that made suburbanization possible. Nonetheless, it was the land speculators who were able to excite the community about the potential of the district.

The Devil's Backbone or, as it is now called, Lowry Hill, was the first section of the lake district to be platted into blocks and lots. The consortium responsible for the registry of the plat in October 1872 included Thomas Lowry, his father-in-law C. G. Goodrich, William

Woodbridge McNair, and the Herrick brothers, W. W. and Edwin W. These were extraordinary men, described in flowery Victorian language by Atwater as pillars of society and industry.

Lowry's contribution to the city has already been described. His father-in-law, C. G. Goodrich, was a physician who made a fortune investing in real estate. According to Atwater, "few men have lived and died in Minneapolis or elsewhere, leaving behind them more reminiscences of kindly services done to their fellows." Goodrich died in 1880 at the age of sixty and so did not live to see the fullfillment of his planned developments.

W. W. McNair was an incredible fellow who was described as a "most enthusiastic and efficient participant in public enterprises, a leader at the bar and, above all, one whose vivacity of disposition, honorable life and genial companionship endeared him to all who knew him." It would seem as though McNair was a perfect politician and participated in many activities of a quasi-public nature. Although he was a democrat, then the minority party in the state, he was elected mayor of Saint Anthony and when he ran for state-wide office, he carried Minneapolis but lost in the rural republican districts. He was involved in several major corporations, including the Minneapolis Gas Light Company, the Minneapolis Street

Railway Company and the Minneapolis and Saint Louis Railway. He also bought timber lands and even acquired a sawmill. An avid outdoorsman and conservationist, he was able to reap a great profit from enterprises that were necessary for the growth of the city and the development of the state's resource base. After years of overwork, he died in 1885, leaving his widow ensconced in a tremendous stone mansion at 1301 Linden Ave., to enjoy what was reputed to be the largest estate ever left by a professional man.

The final two members of the group were the Herricks, capitalists who came to Minneapolis from upstate New York by way of Ohio. Having made a sizable fortune in trade further east, they came to the frontier to invest in real estate and resources. In addition to the development of suburban areas, they built and managed downtown commercial buildings.

The Groveland Addition

The Groveland Addition, platted by this consortium, comprised nearly all the western section of Minneapolis. Lowry Hill was about in the middle of the tract. The addition contained several neighborhoods. Along the railroad tracks at the northern edge of the addition, cheap housing was built to house workers. Industrial activities were expected to locate in this section of the addition along the rails. The development also contained extensive hilltop estates. Lowry's own house was built on a 4.35 acre estate, labelled lot A on the plat map.

Lowry's decision to live in this area was instrumental in its establishment as a prestigious neighborhood rivaling the older, less suburban area around Fair Oaks. It is clear that Lowry expected great things from this plat because he and his father-in-law retained sole possession of a large piece of land lying to the west of Lowry Hill. They obviously expected to plat this portion of land at a later time when the land values were higher. The parcel was eventually sold to the Reverend Henry Beard, another real estate developer who platted it as the Summit Park Addition in 1878.

Isaac Casper Seeley was yet another in the series of colorful individuals engaged in land development. Seeley came to Minneapolis in 1872 as an insurance agent, after a remarkable set of experiences as a cavalry soldier in the Union Army. The insurance business was just then beginning to influence the financial world of the nineteenth century, and Seeley was in a position to profit by its early growth. He gradually withdrew from insurance, however, and in 1880 his company engaged in real estate loans and insurance. He and his partners were able to guide the growth of Minneapolis during the boom years by determining who received loans. Seeley also engaged in resort development on Minnetonka and maintained an extensive country estate — a 2000 acre stock farm in Lyon County. By 1890 he had erected over 100 houses and stores in various parts of the city.

Kenwood: An Early Suburb

The company's 95-acre Kenwood Addition had all the charm and convenience required by the discriminating residents it sought to attract. Early advertisements described it as "high, sightly, attractive" and "less than half the distance to the southern edge of the city." The company unhesitatingly proclaimed it the "choicest place for elegant residences." The success of this development was assured by restrictions. The area was located on some of the most scenic land in the city, it was traversed by boulevards, and no house was to be built for less than $3000. The land around Lake of the Isles had just been purchased for a park and city services were being established. The streetcar lines were on their way. In the meantime the Minneapolis and Saint Louis Railroad provided an ornamental station at Twenty-first Street to shelter commuters while they waited by the tracks. The key to the neighborhood was, however, its elevation. Until Lake of the Isles was dredged, its marshy shoreline was a handicap. Kenwood was free from all of the lakeside inconveniences and was nearly totally built up by 1900 (See tour of Kenwood, p. 86).

The Island Park Addition to Minneapolis was made in 1886 on the west side of the Lake of the Isles. This plat was filed well in advance of the great improvements in the character of the lake made by the dredging and landscaping activities of the park board. As a result, the fifty to fifty-five foot lots in this neighborhood did not attract a stable middle class population until after the turn of

William W. McNair (J. H. Kent, Minnesota Historical Society).

the century. But by the start of World War I it was occupied by a population much better off than their neighbors across Hennepin, yet not ashamed to ride the streetcar downtown. These people were to reap the greatest benefits of the park system, for their homesites would, in all probability, have remained unoccupied had the lake not been improved.

During the 1880s all the land in the lake district north of Lake Street was divided into blocks and lots. The area was designed to provide homes for a variety of households wishing to take advantage of both the physical beauty of the neighborhoods, as well as the convenience afforded by the streetcar lines.

The hilltop locations in the north were developed for affluent families who could afford the higher construction and maintenance costs. The boulevards along Hennepin and Lyndale were also attractive to the upper middle class and a few mansions were constructed there before the century came to a close. Residents from the older districts, closer to downtown or across the river in old Saint Anthony, relocated in the fine houses in the eastern section of the Groveland Addition and along Hennepin. A few prosperous families such as the Glueks were attracted to the Wedge where they built imposing houses.

Nineteenth Century Hennepin Avenue

Like many other businessmen who prospered during the eighties and nineties, J. M. Griffith sought to get away from the crowding of the older sections of the city. In 1898 he moved his family into a fine house on the corner of Twenty-second and Hennepin. Writing many years later, his son reminisced about the move and the house:

> In 1898, when I was 16 years old, our family moved from the old home on 1101 Fifth Street North to a new and splendid house that Father had built at 2220 Hennepin Avenue in southwest Minneapolis. Hennepin Avenue, then, from the Thomas Lowry home at the top of Lowry Hill to Lake Street, was the main thoroughfare through a fine residential district.
>
> The distinction of the neighborhood was not spoiled by the streetcar tracks that ran on Hennepin, for these made a kind of boulevard in themselves. They were

elevated about six inches above street level and had a smooth green carpet of grass growing between them and alongside.

At the time we moved there, only one other house, the Winter home, fronted on Hennepin between 22nd and 24th Streets. All the property behind us as far as the Lake of the Isles was farm land and the lake was then an unimproved swamp with marshy shores.

Our new house, a large one, reflected Father's success and wealth; he was now 65 and retired, and he had paid for the house as it was being built. It boasted of two status symbols of the time — a ballroom on the third floor and a conservatory on the main floor. There were six bedrooms and a bathroom on the second floor, six rooms on the first floor and a large curved plateglass window in the parlor facing Hennepin. The basement had a laundry, bathroom, storage room and a furnace room equipped with a huge tubular hot water boiler.

In back were a spacious stable and outdoor pen for three horses, a cow and chickens, a storage shed for wagons and buggies, and an upstairs loft for hay. This latter was equipped with a pulley to haul up straw and hay bales.

In the early twentieth century the lots of Russell's subdivision on the southeast shore of Lake of the Isles attracted settlers. Russell, like most of the other promoters, envisioned a grandiose neighborhood. His plans called for houses on landscaped isles connected to the mainland by a causeway. Like the others, he eventually settled for less, and sold out to the park board.

Soon apartment buildings for the wealthy were built along Hennepin, and the street became a monumental boulevard. These fine buildings complemented the private mansions of such residents as the Lowry, Donaldson and Partridge families.

Southern Neighborhoods

In contrast to the orderly process of subdivision that characterized the portion of the district north of Lake Street, the land around Lake Calhoun was involved in a complex web of promotions, lawsuits, dreams and schemes before it was finally developed. It provided the home for Cloudman's people when they attempted to

Kenwood Parkway viewed from Queen Avenue in 1906. The blurred figures on the sidewalk are carrying umbrellas (Luxton, Minnesota Historical Society).

The Kenwood depot of the Minneapolis and St. Louis Railroad in 1893, located at the end of West 21st Street (Wallof, Minnesota Historical Society).

House and wood pile at 2925 Lyndale in 1890 (Baltuff, Minnesota Historical Society).

transform their lifestyle. Later it was the site of the grandiose country estate of Colonel William S. King and provided elegant resort hotels for the wealthy. The beauty and accessibility of the place attracted the attention of nearly every real estate developer. It seems that this lake was the pivotal place in the evolution of the city. The group that could carry out a development scheme here would be enormously wealthy.

The story begins with King and his famous Lyndale Farm. Although he was regarded as a wealthy man, it seems he over-extended himself when he bought the claims and farms around the west shore of Lake Harriet and Lake Calhoun in the late 1860s and early 1870s, borrowing heavily. An influential member of the community with a promising career ahead of him, most men thought loaning him money was a good risk. Among the men who loaned King money was a shadowy eastern financier named Philo Remington. In 1878 or 1879, King ran into serious financial trouble and lost control of his property.

While King was planning his estate, his neighbor across the lake, Louis Menage, was making plans of quite a different sort. Menage was perhaps the most colorful of all the real estate adventurers active in the development of Minneapolis. In many respects the career of this transplanted New Englander is typical of frontier entrepreneurs. But not all men were as adventurous nor, it would seem, as unlucky.

Menage was born in Providence, Rhode Island. After spending his boyhood in New Bedford, Massachusetts, he came to Minneapolis in 1871 as a young man to seek the benefit of Minnesota's salubrious climate. Menage had lung problems and, like many other people from the East and South during that era, was lured to Minnesota by the exaggerated claims made about the state's invigorating climate. He was apparently well-educated because he taught shorthand at a local commercial college. His health improved to the point where he was strong enough to spend the following two winters in a north woods logging camp working as a clerk and timekeeper. During the intervening summer he was placed in charge of the wood department at one of the sawmills at Saint Anthony Falls. He appears to have saved his money. Up

The J. M. Griffith house was built at 22nd and Hennepin as a suburban villa in 1889 (H. L. Griffith, Minneapolis, the New Sawdust Town, 1968).

Louis Menage, one of the city's most colorful developers, platted much of the lake district in addition to investing in the Lyndale Hotel and downtown office buildings (Isaac Atwater, History of Minneapolis, *1893).*

to this point his career follows a familiar pattern — a well-educated young man comes to the frontier where his skills in communication and figuring are in great demand in all facets of the booming local economy.

In 1873 or 1874, Menage took a big step and together with a partner opened a real estate office in an older part of downtown Minneapolis at First and Washington. As business grew, he relocated to the new Nicollet House, and his partner retired. Menage was active in many forms of financing and real estate dealings and was one of the leading developers of suburban property to the west of Minneapolis during the late 1870s and 1880s. His pattern was to buy, either alone or in partnership, large blocks of farmland just beyond the zone of active subdivision. He would then plat these areas into blocks and lots and market them. Some of his more well-known additions are Windom's, Prospect Park, Bloomington Avenue, Lake Side Park, Cottage City, and some of the Remington Additions in the vicinity of Lake Calhoun.

Menage's first real estate venture in the lake district had been the platting of his property on the west side of Lake Calhoun in December 1874, known as Menage's Lake Side Park. As we have seen, his attempt to develop a resort hotel on this site failed because people were more interested in either King's Pavilion on the east side of the lake or the more rural settings of Lake Minnetonka. Menage felt the west side of Calhoun was ideally suited for extensive suburban estates. With all of its lots larger than those on Lowry Hill, Lake Side Park was expected to appeal to the very wealthy who would be able to commute to Minneapolis in their personal carriages. There were several stupendous lots, with over 200 feet of lake frontage. Others were located on high ground and had a commanding view of the district. As can be seen on the 1874 map, the land was well beyond the area served by good roads, railroads or street railroads. Only the road now known as Excelsior Avenue served this area. It is doubtful if any lots were sold to people with intentions of building houses on them.

However, Menage was able to interest speculative investors in the property. In 1891 it was replatted as Mendoza Park. Although there were only fifty-eight lots in the first development, Mendoza Park had over 550! Menage had seen the light. Lake Calhoun was not to be the home of the super rich. He planned to make an even greater profit by selling smaller lots and enticing the lower income householders to the area.

His expanding business led to the incorporation of the Northwest Guaranty Loan Company. This firm, along with other business, took care of the financing for people wishing to buy property from Menage. Among the Guaranty Company's board members were the Pillsburys, Washburn and Lowry. The firm boasted of assets totaling $4 million in 1892 and conducted business throughout the United States and abroad.

Menage was also the principal shareholder in the company that owned and managed the Guaranty Loan Building. This twelve story, granite office block, located on the corner of Third Street and Second Avenue South was later called the Metropolitan Building. It housed in sumptuous offices two banks, the headquarters of a railroad and nearly all the leading law firms of the era. In addition, there were bathrooms in the basement, cafes for men and ladies, as well as a general dining room. In fine weather a string orchestra played for dinners on the rooftop pavilion. Menage owned the IDS Tower of the early 1890s.

Even though Menage was one of the leading financiers of the city, and together with his wife Amanda hosted the "Season" for the newly rich Minneapolis society at their resort on Calhoun, he was described as a quiet man who could sit "amidst this bewildering rush of business, surrounded by so much architectural beauty and convenience. . . . the most unpretentious and modest of all the thronging multitude."

Menage's world came apart at the seams during the panic of 1893. His company was wiped out and he was indicted for fraud. Menage, the man who helped found the city's first hospital, a supporter of nearly every civic, charitable and scientific cause, fled to Guatemala rather than face the humiliation of a public trial. Eventually the charges against him were annulled and he returned to the United States. However, he did not return to Minneapolis and apparently had little influence on the city's subsequent development.

The Subdivision of the King Estate

An intricate web of legal and financial dealings covers the development of King's property on the east side of Calhoun. We have seen that King had greatly overextended his financial resources and in 1877 gave up his Pavilion on the lake. In either 1877 or 1878 he wrote a deed for his property to Philo Remington. In return for the deed, Remington paid off several claims against the land. Not long after that, Remington's affairs took an unexpected turn for the worse, and he requested repayment from King. King was unable to redeem his deed, and Remington's agents and lawyers decided to subdivide the land and sell lots. King was left with only the area around his farmstead. Thus began one of the most sensational lawsuits that the legal community of that time had witnessed. King argued that he had not given title of the land to Remington but that the deed was given in trust. While the lawyers from Minneapolis and

New York wrangled, the land was divided. All the land north of the cemetery to Lake Street, as well as the area around Lake Harriet was platted. These areas were then resold to local investors.

The area on the east side of the lake between Lakewood Cemetery and Lake Street was divided into two separate tracts. One, called Lyndale, lay to the west of Hennepin. The other, called Remington's Second Addition, comprised the area between Hennepin and Lyndale. The motorline station, the extensive grounds around the Pavilion and the new hotel, prompted Remington to design Lyndale as a garden suburb, complete with curved streets and large lots.

In 1882, Louis Menage bought 1157 acres of the Lyndale Farm from Remington's agents. Menage must have known that the title on this land was clouded but decided to take a risk on the outcome of the case. His experience on the west side of Calhoun convinced him that the lake would not become an elite railroad suburb. He replatted the section of land on the east shore of the lake called Lyndale. The streets of the grand suburb Remington had envisioned had not been graded, and so Menage simply caused a new plat to be drawn and called the area Calhoun Park. In the process he increased the number of lots ten times. His middle class Calhoun Park, with grid pattern streets so characteristic of the rest of South Minneapolis, replaced the genteel railroad suburb of Remington.

In a related project, Menage platted Cottage City in 1882. This area was also divided into very small lots. The development was served by a wagon road to Richfield and was expected to attract a large population of householders who wished to live near the water but could not afford one of the larger lots being developed on other shores.

Menage built streets and caused the street railway to be extended to serve the eastern sections of his projects. Many lots were sold and clusters of houses began to spring up on various locations. In 1885, the process was brought to a halt by the action of the Minnesota Supreme Court, which, in upholding the decision of the lower courts, awarded the land and damages to King. Menage turned over to King securities, property and cash totaling $2 million. Contemporary accounts would have us believe this action neither affected his financial standing nor ruffled his serenity.

In the late 1880s, Bryn Mawr was platted and a few changes in the older plat were made, but the pattern of the neighborhoods had been fixed. The dreams of great country houses shared by King, Remington and Menage came to nothing. Lowry Hill and Kenwood attracted the social elite but the rest of the lake district was platted into middle class housing districts with a complete range of commercial services.

The Development of the Business Community

Although the railroads on the northwestern edge of the district attracted industrial developments in the early 1880s, no retail or wholesale trade took place in the district until 1885. By that time the street railway and real estate promoters had attracted enough people to the new developments to provide a market for small merchants.

In 1885 there were three clusters of business enterprises. One was located north of the Hennepin-Lyndale intersection, the second and largest was at the corner of Lyndale and Lake, and the smallest centered near the corner of Lake and Hennepin. A handful of businesses operated out of people's homes scattered throughout the area as well. In total there were thirty-one commercial operations in the district. They all provided goods and services that residents of the area needed frequently. Because most, if not all of their customers walked, businesses served a small area. Their profitability was directly related to the popularity and honesty of the proprietor.

The Lyndale-Lake cluster was the largest because this was a junction of the primary north-south and east-west routes. More people went past or transferred at this corner than at any other in the area. There was also a cluster of houses in the vicinity. Both these factors contributed to the intersection's early importance.

There were very few people living in the western section of the district at this time. Consequently only a few merchants could make a living at the Hennepin and Lake intersection. The great land boom and the population

Cottage City was designed to provide summer houses and modest homes on Calhoun's south shore (Minnesota Historical Society).

This cottage at 3823 Vincent Avenue was built for $600 in 1914.

*Witt's market, 2210 Hennepin, in the 1930s; the building
is now Rasmussen Import (Minneapolis Public Library).*

*Russell T. Lund, founder of Lunds, Inc., standing behind
the crackers at Hove's where he began as a clerk in
the 1920s (Lunds, Inc.).*

*A Hupmobile agency, 1645 Hennepin, one of
many auto dealers located on Hennepin during the 1920s
(Minnesota Historical Society).*

growth in the northern sections of the district had caused a near doubling of the number of businesses by the end of the decade.

During the early 1890s, the Lyndale Avenue commercial district came into full flower. The total number of businesses in the district increased from fifty-two in 1890 to ninety-two in 1895. Fifty-two of these were either on or within two blocks of Lyndale Avenue. The Lake Street intersection was still the largest concentration. Drugstores, hardware stores, grocers, and meat markets did a thriving business. By 1895, they were located on nearly every intersection between Lake Street and the city center. Feed stores, dry goods merchants and flour dealers also established themselves here. Physicians, nurses and accountants moved in above grocers, barbers and meat markets. A large number of women entered the business community during this decade, operating dress shops and millineries or giving music lessons in their homes.

The area around the Chicago, Milwaukee and Saint Paul railroad tracks on Twenty-ninth Street attracted light manufacturing unwilling to pay the high rents demanded downtown. Manufacturers of medicine, carriages and harnesses provided employment for area residents. In addition, dealers in fuel, stoves, home appliances, and marble for grave monuments found Lyndale a good business location.

The electrification of the streetcar lines and the growth of the Lowry Hill and Kenwood neighborhoods brought many more prosperous people into the area. However, businesses could not really take advantage of the growth in the western section of the district because commercial buildings were prohibited on Hennepin, which was maintained by the park board as a boulevard until 1905. By 1900 the large number of people living in apartment houses was demanding goods and services unavailable locally. This prompted the establishment of retail stores in the western section of the Wedge, with a few entrepreneurs bold enough to ignore park board restrictions locating on Hennepin.

During the first decade of the twentieth century, the streetcar lines promoted the dispersal of a large number of commercial enterprises out of downtown. A part of this

By 1920 commercial buildings like these on Lake Street just west of Lyndale dominated major thoroughfares of the district, providing the local residents with a wide range of goods and services (Minneapolis Public Library).

41

trend was the establishment of several professional offices on Hennepin Avenue. The economic and political structure of the city was becoming more complex, and people needed lawyers to bring them through a myriad of legal problems. Architects, engineers and real estate agents who assisted in the building boom at the turn of the century found the new office space on prestigious Hennepin Avenue ideally suited to their needs. All enjoyed easy access to the center of the city and the proximity of one of the leading residential districts in the city. Like the dentists and doctors, they found the second floor offices of the commercial buildings "made to order."

The Hennepin-Lake Intersection

During the Twenties, the Lake and Hennepin intersection, where large buildings were built at the turn of the century, grew to rival the older core at Lake and Lyndale. Its proximity to Lake Calhoun gave it a special atmosphere — not quite a resort area but certainly a special shopping district. Further north on Hennepin the process of replacement began. Vacant corner lots were taken over by commercial buildings. Duplexes and other multiple family structures were built facing the street,

and some of the early residential structures were occupied by people who worked out of their homes.

A streetcar commuter returning home to south Minneapolis in 1930 would find a tight cluster of stores and offices at the Hennepin-Lake transfer line, with a selection of goods and services that would satisfy one's every need.

Large commercial buildings provided imposing facades on each corner of the intersection. A tired shopper could relax with a cherry coke at Walgreen's, which established a branch on the southeast corner and rivaled Louis Liggett's drugstore across the street. Abdallah's on the northwest corner attracted people with a sweet tooth, serving ice cream and peddling delight-filled hand-dipped chocolates, and assorted hard candies.

Working women could purchase on the corner everything needed for the family's dinner. The American Fruit Store on the northeast corner displayed local truck farmer's produce. John Schmidler's meat store on the same corner sold only meat in an era when grocers sold none. Other food items could be purchased up Hennepin at Hove's, the forerunner of today's Lund's.

A different perspective of the street crossing was afforded to clients of doctors and lawyers in offices located

Abdallah's dominated the northwest corner of Hennepin and Lake in the 1930s (Roth, Minneapolis Public Library).

above the street level shops. Glancing from a waiting room window a client would look down on the crisscross maze of streetcar electric lines and the colorful striped shop awnings. After five o'clock storeowners rolled up these awnings, merchants brought in produce stands and the softly-lit streetlights glowed.

Passersby, looking for an evening's entertainment, could munch Kits Korn Krib popcorn at 2904 Hennepin while reading the marquee of the Lagoon Theater next door. This theater showed silent movies in the teens and changed its name to the Uptown in 1929 with the inauguration of its first talkies. If they were hungry, they could choose between egg rolls at the Kin Chu Cafe or Greek specialties at the New Rainbow Cafe, opened in 1919. Owner Christ Legerose was a zealous art patron, as well, and provided space on his restaurant's walls for local artists to show their work.

By 1925 the nature of the business community throughout the district was established. New commercial buildings replaced old residential structures on Hen-

nepin Avenue. New types of businesses were attracted to the avenue because it remained the major route through the residential districts of southwest Minneapolis. Stores selling "notions," beauty shops, clothing stores, and dry cleaners all found the densely settled middle class neighborhoods on either side of Hennepin an ideal market. The street was changed into a stop and shop district. Everyone seemed to be making money.

Car dealers, moving away from the congestion in downtown, were attracted to Hennepin, as well. By 1930, the area around the bottleneck had developed into one of the city's earliest auto rows. It was lined with car dealers, repair shops and dealers in auto accessories. The old manufacturing district along Twenty-ninth Street maintained itself, but everyone realized it would not expand into a sizable industrial area.

During this decade, Hennepin replaced Lyndale as the primary commercial area in the district and began to provide goods and services for clientele spread over the entire city. Between 1920 and 1930 the number of businesses with a clientele from outside the neighborhoods more than doubled. This was a major change in the nature of the business community. What had begun as a service area for the immediate neighborhood expanded to become one of the major shopping and entertainment districts of the city.

Schlampp's is a good example of this sort of company. Established in 1905, it is one of the oldest retail businesses at Hennepin and Lake. Its founder emigrated to Minneapolis from Germany and brought with him the expertise and knowledge of the furrier's trade. Schlampp's was first located in north Minneapolis, then a thriving business district that rivaled the downtown area. He apparently foresaw Hennepin and Lake's tremendous commercial growth and moved his business there in the early twenties. The original Schlampp building on Hennepin and Lake with its elaborate facade, was constructed in 1922 by Pesek and Shifflet, a well-known architectural team.

In response to the financial needs of the growing commercial community at the Lake and Hennepin intersection, the Fifth Northwestern Bank was established in 1927. The bank was managed by Clarence Hill, a life-long resident of south Minneapolis. The Calhoun State Bank opened on Lake Street in the Twenties to tap the financial strength of burgeoning residential and business communities.

The large number of people living east of Hennepin in rooming houses without kitchen privileges provided a modest but reliable market for restaurants on Hennepin and Lake. These small enterprises, generally based upon the resources and labor of single families, tended to be short-lived.

Increased leisure time, the perfection of the talking movies and the convenience of streetcar transportation combined to make movie theaters one of the most profitable business enterprises in the 1920s and 1930s. During these years, the number of movie houses increased dramtically, and neighborhood theaters were built along the streetcar lines in every corner of the city. In 1913 the Lagoon Theater opened; in 1929 its name was changed to the Uptown. This name change indicates the changing perception of the lake district. It was becoming known as a sophisticated and integral part of the city, no longer a rural retreat. The Granada Theater, now the Suburban World, opened in 1928. Like thousands of theaters across the country with the same name, it was designed to exploit the nation's passion for the mysterious desert culture of the Moors, popularized by Rudolph Valentino. The movie business was prosperous throughout the Depression and war years but could not compete for the mass audience once television sets were affordable.

The 1920s and early 1940s were halycon days for small businessmen and women in the lake district. Although a tremendous spurt of growth accompanied the first wave of settlement between 1900 and 1910, it was greatly overshadowed by the enormous growth of the teens and twenties. The 278 businesses added to the area in those years were established to serve the middle class families filling in the densely built neighborhoods associated with the streetcar lines. The Twenties were an extremely prosperous decade and over 400 new establishments served the community at the end of the decade, a remarkable 82 percent increase.

The Great Depression dealt the community of small businesses a staggering blow. Customers could not pay bills and creditors foreclosed on establishment after establishment over the city. But the basic stability of the

Above left, Lakeland Academy, 1402 W. Lake, originally the Calhoun Theatre (Western Architect);
the Granada (1928) is now the Suburban World (Minneapolis Public Library).
Below, the east side of Hennepin Avenue near Lake Street in 1925 (Minnesota Historical Society).

45

A district landmark as it looked in 1963; now the Calhoun Beach Club, it is the only survivor of many Lake Calhoun resort hotels (Minnesota Historical Society).

residential area meant that the well-run businesses could survive the hard years. By the end of the decade their number was on the rise again. One hundred and thirty-six additional businesses were in operation at the end of the decade.

After World War II, the character of the commercial community was drastically altered. The widespread availability of automobiles caused the city population to disperse to the suburbs, and the population of the lake district began to level off and then decline. The streets of the lake district became thoroughfares for commuters. The businesses along Hennepin and Lyndale became increasingly oriented toward automobile traffic. The large plate glass display windows that once lured pedestrians and people riding streetcars were replaced by large signs that were easier for passing motorists to read. Businesses lost their clientele to suburban shopping centers. Some businesses followed the customers to the shopping centers after a few years; others stayed and, joined by new members, are forging a new future with the changing population of the district.

Churches and Synagogues

Eighteen churches and synagogues have been organized in the lake district, and thirteen of them still exist — a very high rate of perseverance.

The two oldest congregations in the area are the Lyndale Congregational Church, now located at 810 West Thirty-first Street, but originally established in 1884 on Lake Street at Aldrich; and the Joyce Memorial Methodist Church, now located on Thirty-first and Fremont, but first organized on Lake Street at Fremont in 1886. This seems ironic today, since there are presently no neighborhood churches located on Lake Street with the exception of the Salvation Army at 1516 West Lake. The Third Church of Christ Scientist, once located on Lake and Humboldt, has also moved.

The favorite location for churches and synagogues has been Hennepin Avenue. The Basilica of Saint Mary, the Cathedral of Saint Mark, and the Hennepin Avenue Methodist Church all lie just outside the borders of the lake district but close enough to provide places of worship for many neighborhood residents. All three are located on or just off Hennepin Avenue. Lowry Hill Congregational Church, now disbanded, was built in 1902 at the tip of the Wedge where the freeway now turns. The Sixth Church of Christ Scientist and the Trinity Community Church (originally Baptist) are both located just off Hennepin at Summit and Lincoln avenues.

Fowler Methodist Church was built on Franklin and Dupont at the turn of the century and then merged with the congregation at Hennepin Avenue Methodist, the building being converted to the Scottish Rite Temple.

Temple Israel moved to their present location at Twenty-fourth Street and Emerson, facing Hennepin, when there was only a nineteenth century residence there. Their present temple was constructed in 1928.

Grace Presbyterian Church is located across from West High School, on Twenty-eighth and Humboldt, quite near Hennepin Avenue.

Other than Lake and Hennepin locations, there are only six other churches in the lake district. Three congregations in the north section have been established relatively recently. The Unitarian Society is located at 900 Mount Curve, Lake of the Isles Lutheran at Twenty-first and West Lake of the Isles Boulevard, and Saint Paul's Episcopal Church (located in 1901 quite close to Hennepin at Franklin and Bryant) has now moved to Franklin and Morgan.

South of Lake Street are located Saint Mary's Greek Orthodox Church built in 1972 at 3500 South Irving, the Adath Yeshurun synagogue at Thirty-fourth Street and Dupont, and the Aldrich Avenue Presbyterian Church on the corner of Thirty-fifth Street.

Below, left, Temple Israel worshipped in this house, later building their synagogue on the same site (Minnesota Historical Society) Below, right, Joyce Memorial Methodist Church in 1905 (Minnesota Historical Society).

Before this picture was considered suitable for publication, a censor obscured the girl's bare knees in this 1908 bathing scene at Lake Calhoun (Minnesota Historical Society).

CHAPTER 4

Life on the Lakes

Wide, wooden, green-painted steps led down our wooded bank to the lake, and halfway there was "the landing" with seats on either side. Oh, the lovely western sunsets from that landing in the evening! The black tamarack forest pointed up into them. When the lake was yellow glass in the evening, my parents and their friends would row on it. Their voices lifted up so purely and beautifully, mingling from one boat to another, in "Good Night, Ladies." It came over the water with the slow, musical clunk of the oarlocks.

That recollection from the turn of the century seems to capture the eternal presence of the lakes. Wherever you are in the Calhoun-Isles neighborhood, you sense the lakes. And whoever you are, you can wander down to the dock at the foot of Lake Street and rent a canoe, paddle out into that same sun-gilt twilight scene, and — even sing if you please! Life on the lakes does not change. So we think, and so we deceive ourselves. The lakes have always been the focus of the area, the focus for the whole city for that matter. But the way the lakes have been used has changed in virtually every decade.

However, there has never been a settler by these shores who did not think the lakes were beautiful. Although the Indians left us no descriptive literature, we know they loved the lakes. The siting of Cloudman's village, near perhaps the prettiest spot on the shore of Lake Calhoun, cannot have been an accident. The lake provided fish, water fowl, and drinking water for the Indians and fed their need for beauty.

The first white settlers used the lakes in the same way. One of the earliest housewives in Saint Anthony recalled:

> A Mr. Mosseau, who lived on Lake Calhoun, had a son who brought us ducks and fish for two or three years. He was a clever youngster, not yet in his teens when he first came, but must have been a skillful sportman, for he nearly always brought us splendid redheads and mallards, and also the largest and finest fish.

This same woman remembered that Calhoun and Harriet became favorite fishing haunts as soon as the army redrew the boundaries for Fort Snelling in 1845.

Even though the wild geese still swim on Lake of the Isles and ducks nest on its islands, it is hard to imagine what these lakes must have been like when the first settlers enjoyed their beauty. Their descriptions remind one of the Garden of Eden:

> In many places the trees were literally impurpled by

Ice harvesting in the
lake district: cutting,
storing, and delivering the
blocks of ice (Minnesota
Historical Society).

The west shore of Cedar Lake in 1885 (Scott, Hennepin County Historical Society).

the masses of grapes; plums and cherries were equally abundant, and of berries, especially strawberries, there was no end. On the north shore of Calhoun there was a bed of the latter of more than an acre in extent, in which one could hardly set foot without crushing the berries. Wagon loads of people from town used to resort there, and return laden with bushels of the luscious fruit. On the south shore of Harriet may still be seen the scattered progeny of the fruit, which, in that early time, flushed the banks with scarlet and filled the air with delicious fragrance.

Even the more sober and scientific Henry David Thoreau seemed to have been overcome with the wild variety of species he discovered around the lakes during his brief journey to Minnesota in 1861. The ailing writer and naturalist made only fragmentary entries in his notebooks and never wrote any connected account of his visit to the neighborhood, but his cryptic comments do provide some fascinating insights. "As much as the stabler can do to get rid of his manure," he writes. "Wheat

often grows too stout as it is." He fished and watched the loons as he did at Walden Pond fifteen years earlier. He thought he might have discovered a new variety of oriole. He identified a familiar honeysuckle (*lonicera parviflora*), noting that it grew two to ten feet high in Minnesota. But he also brusquely remarked, "Myriads of musquitoes. Wood ticks." And he noted the changes that were already taking place at Lake Calhoun. Walking along the east shore he listened to the song of the horned lark and watched the killdeer's antics. He had evidently heard about the Pond brothers' exploits, and was searching for signs of their cabin. He noted the "site of Pond's mission overgrown with sumach and covered with gopher heaps."

Ice Harvesting

When winter came to the lakes, their beauty did not die nor did their usefulness. Even as they were appreciated for their summer bounty of fish, game, and fruits, so too was the winter ice mined like a mineral. As early as the 1880s, the Boston Ice Company and the Cedar Lake Ice Company both built sets of rather ramshackle buildings on the north shore of Lake Calhoun about 800 feet west of the Calhoun-Isles bridge. They stood there until removed by the park board in 1909, an action "welcomed by the entire population of the city," Theodore Wirth asserted. Those structures probably never would have been marked for preservation by the Minneapolis Heritage Preservation Commission, but the cutting of the ice certainly seems to have been a picturesque occupation. Henry David Thoreau would have recognized that side of life on Lake Calhoun, too, since he had watched the ice "miners" at work on Walden Pond.

> While yet it is cold January, and snow and ice
> are thick and solid, the prudent landlord comes
> from the village to get ice to cool his summer drink;
> impressively, even pathetically wise, to foresee the heat
> and thirst of July now in January, — wearing a thick
> coat and mittens! when so many things are not provided
> for. It may be that he lays up no treasures in this world
> which will cool his summer drink in the next. He cuts
> and saws the solid pond, unroofs the house of fishes,
> and carts off their very element and air, held fast by
> chains and stakes like corded wood, through the
> favoring winter air, to wintry cellars, to underlie the
> summer there. It looks like solidified azure, as, far off,
> it is drawn through the streets. These ice-cutters are a
> merry race, full of jest and sport, and when I went
> among them they were wont to invite me to saw
> pit-fashion with them, I standing underneath.

One wonders whether the same Boston Ice Company which settled on Lake Calhoun might not have been at work on Walden Pond.

Ice was needed not only in the family ice boxes and in the coolers of the grocery and meat shops, but it was also in demand for cooling the refrigerator cars that carried perishable food products. The proximity of the railroad to Lake Calhoun certainly dictated the location of the ice sheds on the north shore of that lake.

Dredging

In the 1970s property on the shore of any lake in Minneapolis sells for a premium, but in the 1870s, the lakeshore was consciously avoided. The Ponds chose a hilltop thirty feet above the lakeshore. Colonel William S. King and other farmers chose the high ground as well. When Kenwood was platted, only the land well above lake level was built upon. The reason for the remarkable change in settlement patterns is, of course, a remarkable change in the lakes themselves.

Much of the land around Lake Calhoun and Lake of the Isles during the 1880s was described by Wirth as "mosquito-infested, malaria-breeding swamplands." Early photos verify this description. From its earliest organization, the Minneapolis Park Board seems to have chosen the beautification of the lakes as their most important task. For over thirty-five years the park commissioners expended their energies and the city's money to achieve their goal. They virtually remade the landscape.

The dredging process by which this was achieved began on Lake of the Isles in 1889 and was continued until 1893. Before the building of the railroad between Lake Calhoun and Lake of the Isles, the entire area separating the two was a swamp. The railroad began the filling process, creating a right of way over two small hillocks on the south shore of Lake of the Isles that had once formed the third and fourth islands in that lake. Dredging activities by the park board during 1889–93 concentrated mainly upon creating a roadway around the lake and establishing a clearer shoreline on the east. The road was built, but it frequently was flooded during heavy rains or high water.

By 1900 the park board plans were far from complete, and lakeshore residences were still sparse. On Lake Calhoun the only real concentration of settlement had occurred on the high ground on the east side of the lake between Thirty-second and Lake streets where sixteen residences had been built; another dozen (some obviously only cottages) were located on the south shore between Xerxes and Richfield streets; and a third small group of five houses had sprung up just north of the Minikahda Club — thirty-three houses in all. Around the whole Lake of the Isles, there were only six residences, all on the east shore. No one lived on Cedar Lake, and the area south of Twenty-fourth Street, between Cedar and Lake of the Isles, had not even been platted.

During 1907–11, the familiar landscape of Lake of the Isles was created. Half a million cubic yards of fill was

Steam dredges at work at Lake of the Isles in 1909 (Minneapolis Public Library).

dredged out of Lake of the Isles during this period. This operation created Kenilworth Lagoon where only a swamp had existed and made possible the connection between Cedar Lake and Lake of the Isles. The northern-most island in the lake, which during the earlier nineteenth-century dredging operation had been connected to the mainland by a causeway, was again separated. Both islands were enlarged. Wirth estimated that before the dredging, the park board had controlled 100 acres of water, sixty-seven acres of swamp, and only thirty-three acres of dry land at Lake of the Isles. By 1911, there were 120 acres of water and eighty acres of land.

Dredging occurred during two periods at Lake Calhoun, half a million cubic yards of fill being moved in 1911–15, and more than 800,000 cubic yards during 1923–25. Virtually all of the park, beaches and boulevards are built upon man-made land. The three beaches at Thirty-third, Upton and Lake streets, respectively, were created in the earlier period from 1911–15. With the coming of the automobile, the need for all-weather paved roads was recognized, and the dredging of 1923–25 was principally connected with road building. By 1925 the round-the-lakes boulevard system was com-

pleted. By that time the building boom was on; the lakeshore property had been transformed into the asset we now take for granted.

The Linking of the Lakes

In 1906 the park board began to consider dredging canals to link the principal lakes of the district, an idea which seems to have captured the imagination of the public. To join Lake Calhoun to Lake Harriet proved impossible because Harriet was found to be seven feet lower than Calhoun. However, Cedar Lake was not much higher than Lake of the Isles, and Lake of the Isles was virtually the same height as Lake Calhoun. Digging the channels was not very difficult, but the six bridges which were thus made necessary involved expenditure of more than $100,000 by the park board and about half that much by the railroads.

The completion of this project in 1911 was made the occasion of an elaborate and lengthy civic celebration that seems to have anticipated many features of the Aquatennial by thirty years. The fact that today one can canoe or ride a launch (or in earlier years actually swim) from Cedar Lake into Lake of the Isles and then into Lake Calhoun, paddling all the way down to the beach on the south shore, does not seem very exciting to contemporary residents of the district. But in 1911, it proved to be sufficiently historic to rouse virtually the entire city to participate in a week-long ceremony of civic self-congratulation. In a sense the city was celebrating the re-creation of the lakes and the remaking of the landscape.

There is not enough space here even to summarize the activities that were crowded into July 2–8, 1911. Each day was given over to its own ceremonies and named "Homecoming Day," "National Guard Day," "Linking of the Lakes Day," "Historic Pageant Day," "Industrial Day," and "Children's Day." On Wednesday, July 5, "Linking of the Lakes Day," the ceremonies commenced at the bridge nearest to Lake Calhoun, where Lake Street had been closed and a tent had been erected. A small set of gates symbolically blocked entrance to the Lake of the Isles channel. Speeches were delivered, a dedicatory ode recited, water from the two lakes was ritually mixed in a golden loving cup. At that moment the gates were raised and the "Maid of the Isles," bedecked with garlands and flags, passed under the bridge.

That evening Lake of the Isles was the scene of a brilliant parade of illuminated Ships of All Ages, a very beautiful spectacle — novel and educational — in which 170 canoes participated, together with the Women's Rowing Club with a chain of thirty rowboats. A throne had been erected on a platform on the larger of the two islands of the lake, and here five young women in appropriate costumes, impersonating the spirits of Minneapolis, Lake Harriet, Lake of the Isles, Cedar Lake, and Lake Calhoun, reviewed the parade of ships — replicas of ancient water craft illuminated and manned by crews in picturesque historical costumes. The island was also attractively illuminated, and after the water parade, a brilliant display of fireworks climaxed the eventful day.

Launches and Boat Liveries

The linking of the lakes stimulated interest in boating, but did not by any means create that activity. As noted earlier, the Minneapolis, Lyndale, and Minnetonka Railway operated a steamboat on Lake Calhoun, but after that company was merged with Lowry's streetcar lines in 1888, the "Hattie," presumably by then decrepit, was towed into the middle of Lake Calhoun and burned. However, that was not a sign that interest in boating was flagging. The park board encouraged private boating on Lake Calhoun, although the board did order all private docks and bathhouses removed when they gained control of the lakeshore in 1887. Later, dockage and mooring facilities were provided by the board.

The board also in 1889 licensed S. N. Ewing to operate a boat livery at the foot of Thirty-fourth where the old Minnetonka railroad station had been located. Although no photographs of Ewing or his dock seem to have survived, he must have played a well-remembered role in the lives of many residents of the East Calhoun neighborhood, since he continued to operate his concession for more than thirty-five years, 1924 being his last

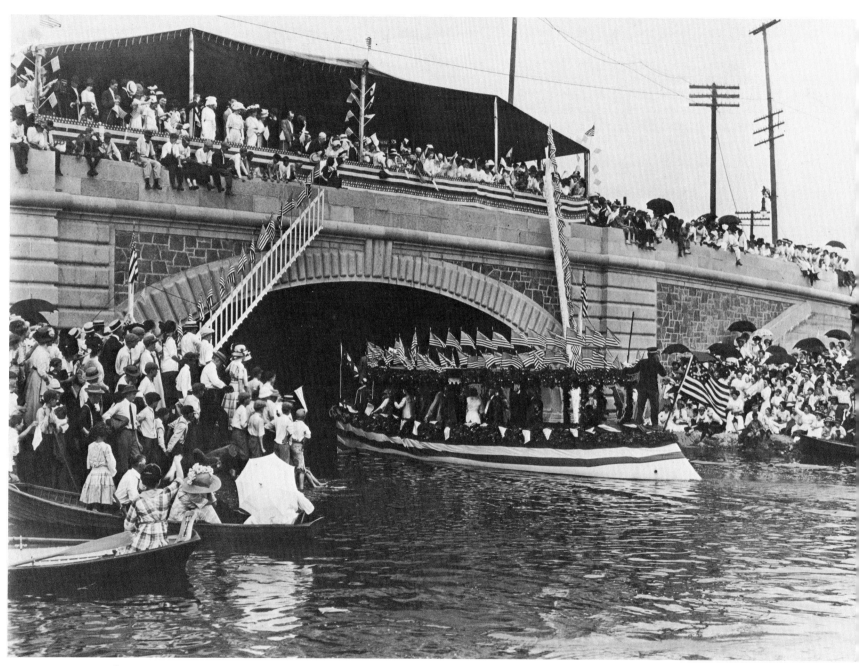

The climactic moment in the celebration of the linking of the lakes; the "Maid of the Isles" sails through the uplifted gates, July 1911. (Hibbard, Minneapolis Park and Recreation Board).

The side-wheeler "Hattie" makes a stop in 1886 on the east side of Lake Calhoun at Thirty-fourth Street (Jewett, Hennepin County Historical Society).

year on the lake. Not only did Ewing rent rowboats, he also operated a steam launch named the "Chief."

After the linking of the lakes, the park board in 1914 purchased two of its own launches, which were powered by gasoline engines. These forty-passenger boats plied regularly scheduled runs around Lake Calhoun and into Lake of the Isles, Cedar Lake, and Brownie Lake. A passenger who boarded one of these launches at the Thirty-first Street dock would have circled Lake Calhoun counterclockwise, stopping at Thirty-fourth Street, Thomas Avenue, Thirty-sixth Street (on the west side of the lake where the stop was named "Mineral Springs"), "Spring Beach" opposite the Minikahda Club, and finally Lake Street. After 1907 the park board also operated its own boat concession, renting thirty rowboats and four sailboats from a ticket booth that stood at the same spot between Lake and Thirty-first streets where in 1978 one can still rent rowboats and sailboats. Some things, at any rate, do not seem to change.

The Sporting Clubs

A great deal of sports activity around the lakes was conducted by clubs. Faithfully reflecting the character of nineteenth century society, these clubs mirrored the class and ethnic divisions existing at that time. In 1887, Minneapolis possessed, for example, a New York Club, for those who themselves or whose ancestors had lived in New York. There also was the Caledonian Club for persons of Scottish ancestry and the Apollo Club whose members were all Jewish.

Sports clubs in the nineteenth century did not vary from that model, and sporting activities would appear to have perpetuated social differences rather than breaking them down. The members of rowing clubs, for example, were usually drawn from socially prominent families. The Lurline Boat Club, which was granted the right to build a boathouse on Lake Calhoun in 1887, the same year the park board gained control of the lake, included among its members Albert C. Loring, son of park board president Charles M. Loring. The Lurline Boat Club's annual receptions were described by an historian of the 1890s as ranking "among the most popular social occa-

Monk's dock on the north shore of Lake Calhoun; the sign on the boat reads, "Across the lake 5¢, trip around the lake 10¢ (Baltuff, Minnesota Historical Society).

sions." Another rowing club, the Lyndale Boat Club, also built a boathouse on Lake Calhoun, but no record of races on the lake seems to have survived. These two boat clubs, of course, competed in racing shells or sculls similar to those used in the famous Harvard-Yale competition, which did so much to popularize the sport with young men.

The Bicycle Mania

Although rowing clubs were quite numerous in the 1880s and 1890s, very few of them have survived into modern times. But as one sports fad waned, another burst upon the scene. In the 1890s, everyone was crazy about cycling.

Bicycles were known in America before the 1890s, but only in the form of the high wheelers. These machines with huge front wheels and tiny rear ones were often called "bone-shakers," since their seats were unsprung and their tires not air-filled. The "safety" bicycle — the machine still popular today — was developed in England about 1885. The pneumatic tire was invented in 1888 by an Irish veterinarian. In 1893, the famous New York six-day bike race was won by Albert Shock riding a safety bicycle.

Soon everyone had become a "wheelman," and cycling clubs had become all the rage. When compared with today's automobile, a bicycle provides only limited mobility. But when compared with a horse or (more commonly) with walking, a bicycle offered greatly enlarged travelling potential. Route maps and member discounts at hotels were arranged for cycle club members. A well-built cycle cost about $50 in 1899.

In order to provide good surfaces for cycling, the Minneapolis Cycle Path Association was organized to raise money for path building and repair. Cyclists were asked to buy a $1 tag. The **Minneapolis Tribune** reported in 1899 about the condition of cycle paths in the lake district:

> An important piece of work as far as cyclists are concerned is the renovation of the boulevards around the lakes and various park sections of the city. These boulevards afford pleasure runs that are the most appreciated of any in the city. The work was commenced by the park board a week ago, and the boulevards around Lake of the Isles, Calhoun, and Harriet are now in very good shape. The cycle path from Lake of the Isles to Lake Calhoun is in the best condition, as is also that through Interlachen and around Lake Harriet.

Traffic became so heavy on city streets that a bicycle inspector was appointed by the mayor to police miscreant

Cyclists lounge beside Peavey Fountain while a sight-seeing coach pauses on its trip around Lake of the Isles (Minneapolis Public Library).

The Tri-Lakes Boat Club war canoe on Lake Calhoun about 1900 (Minnesota Historical Society).

cyclists and also to protect them from coachmen who blocked bicycle paths. The **Tribune** reported on the inspector's activities:

> Scorching on cycle paths has always been a nuisance, and continues with considerable aggravation this year. Bicycle inspector Connor states that the scorcher is a person he is going after hot and heavy. Connor is a hard rider, and knows that he is capable of running the average scorcher to earth.

This mysterious villain, the "scorcher," was the bicycle equivalent of a speeder, usually an aspiring racer who was using city cycle paths as his private track.

Canoe Clubs

Bicycles remained popular until the introduction of automobiles, and, to some extent, they have remained popular ever since, even enjoying something of a renaissance during the 1970s. But in the procession of sporting fads, the canoe emerged in the early twentieth century as the next idol of the public.

Modern canoeing was popularized as early as 1865 by the Scottish sportsman, John MacGregor, who developed a canoe type known as the "Rob Roy," in which he paddled around Europe, Scandinavia, and the eastern Mediterranean. However, MacGregor's was a decked canoe, more similar to modern kayaks. The canoe that became popular in the early twentieth century was an American descendent of the Indians' open birch-bark canoe. Why it became so popular around 1908 is something of a mystery, unless it was because of the addition of flotation chambers to the canoes at that time.

The park board rented that type of "sponson" canoe to the public after 1910. By 1914, canoeing had grown to such an extent that 1,402 canoes were licensed on the six lakes of the park system. Most of them would have been used on Lake Harriet and the Chain of Lakes system. Wirth's description of the canoeing craze reveals as much about his genteel tastes as it does about the customs of the day:

> The owners of private canoes vied with one another in painting their craft in attractive designs and colors, and most of them were labelled with intriguing names and characters. There were times when the canoeing activities became rather troublesome, requiring much patrolling by the police and compelling the board to prohibit any boating on the lakes between midnight

and daylight. Likewise, the board properly refused to issue permits to owners of canoes whose distorted sense of humor caused them to label their craft with suggestive names or designs.

The popularity of the canoe had reached its zenith at the time when the channels between Lake of the Isles, Calhoun and Cedar were first opened. We have already quoted the description of the 170 canoes that participated in the "Linking of the Lakes Day" celebration. The most active canoe club seems to have been organized on Lake Harriet, and the parades of decorated canoes held annually by that club during 1911–16 attracted city-wide interest.

Sailing and the Calhoun Yacht Club

Organized sailing and racing activities on Lake Calhoun were first attempted at the beginning of this century. As early as August 10, 1901, a group of about twenty skippers met to organize the Calhoun Yacht Club, their state charter being issued by the end of that year. Included among the activities that the club sponsored were yacht racing, ice boating, canoe racing, and tennis. The fleet consisted of twenty-five boats including Swallows, Larks, Snipe, and Nationals.

Membership in the club rose to one hundred in the next few years, and sailing competitions were held regularly. But World War I halted all sailing activity. During the 1920s the club was slow to recover its former vigor. Toward the end of that decade national interest in sailing seems to have grown appreciably. The Calhoun Yacht Club experienced a gradual but steady increase of interest in sailboat racing, culminating in the club's admission to the Inland Lakes Yachting Association in 1938.

Contrary to what one would expect, the depression of the 1930s does not seem to have seriously affected sailing activities. Wirth recorded that only ten boats were moored at park board buoys in 1933, but that there were forty-three by 1937; by 1946 that figure had risen to ninety-six.

The Lake of the Isles Driving Club

One of the longest-lived club sports in the lake district was one that is also foreign to our own experience — the sport of horse racing on the frozen surface of Lake of the Isles. Horses, unlike sailboats, cannot be stored during the winter. Whatever the weather, horses need to be exercised if they are to be kept in good condition. Moreover, the horses did not seem to mind cold weather as much as humans. When properly shod with a neverslip shoe equipped with metal cleats or "grabs," the horses not only raced well but seemed sounder of foot at the end of the season than in the autumn. Some horses that had become lame during the dirt track season were cured of their problems by racing on the ice; apparently the natural resilience of the ice and the cushioning effect of the "grabs" contributed to the improvement.

Winter racing did not originate at Lake of the Isles, but it did find its most popular and long-lasting home there. An ice track was built at Lake Calhoun during the first year of the park board's control of the lakes, but it was shifted to Lake of the Isles the next year, and there it stayed (with one year's break) from 1897 through 1929.

A half-mile straight track was laid out, most frequently running east-west across the southern edge of the lake. Snow was removed by horse-drawn plows. At first the drivers were seated on sleighs, but the bicycle-tired sulky was adopted for ice racing in the 1890s at the same time that it became standard equipment for dirt racing. During one year a grandstand was erected, but during most years spectators watched from lakeside. The **Minnesota Horseman** in 1895 reported that:

> The ice track is the best possible location for the spectators as well as the speeders, as it lies quite a bit lower than the boulevard drive where the lookers-on mostly congregate.

Racing was organized by the Lake of the Isles Driving Club, a name changed in the twentieth century to the Minneapolis Driving Club. Races were usually held every Saturday afternoon in the winter, the first race often occurring during Christmas week. Some exceptional horses raced on Lake of the Isles, the best trotters appearing between 1910 and 1920. The most famous

Ice boating on Calhoun about 1901 (Norton and Peel, Minnesota Historical Society).

SCORING FOR THE WORD.

THE 2:17 TROT AT LAKE OF THE ISLES, SATURDAY, JAN. 20.

Jerry L, g. g., 2:17¼, by Stonewall Jackson, Jr., Winner; Clara P., 2:17, by Spink 7627. Second

Top of the page, view to the northeast across the trotting track, skating and hockey rinks on the southeast end of Lake of the Isles in 1916; the Gates mansion is visible on the far left (Hibbard, Minneapolis Park and Recreation Board). Above, an early trotting race on Lake of the Isles (Minnesota Historical Society).

trotter of them all, Dan Patch, did not race at Lake of the Isles, but he did sire several horses that raced for his Minneapolis owner, Marion W. Savage. Savage bought Dan Patch in 1903 for $60,000, and when he was shown publicly for the first time in January 1903, the newspaper reported that "it was necessary to keep a squad of mounted police in advance to clear the street."

The greatest half-mile ever trotted on ice was run by the little stallion, Silver Todd, at Lake of the Isles on February 23, 1920. Owned by F. A. "Ted" Danforth and driven by James Calder, the trotter raced a heat in 59¾ seconds, the only less-than-a-minute ice trot on record.

Although these kinds of records are interesting, it is gratifying to discover that occasionally a horse that was used during the week to pull a carriage or, in one case, a laundry wagon could win a race over horses never used for anything but racing.

Golf and the Minikahda Club

Like horse racing, golf has enjoyed an unusually long period of success. The sport seems to have first become popular in Minneapolis in 1898, during which year not only the Minikahda Club but also the Minneapolis and

Bryn Mawr Clubs were founded. The park board did not introduce golf until 1916. That three private clubs should be founded in Minneapolis in 1898 is all the more impressive when one realizes that the first clubs in the United States were organized only in 1888 and that by 1894 there were still only about a dozen in existence.

The site for the Minikahda Club was chosen, according to the tradition of the club, during a bicycle outing to Lake Calhoun. Two of the cyclists decided the spot on the west side of the lake was ideal for golf. In a later meeting at the West Hotel, the site of many significant gatherings, the club was formally organized by such prominent citizens as Thomas and Horace Lowry, C. G. Goodrich, William H. Dunwoody, and Andreas Ueland. Since the land was still a little beyond the limits of the streetcar lines, the club ran their own launch on shuttle runs from Thirty-first Street to their dock.

The clubhouse was opened in 1899. Designed by F. B.

Above, the Bryn Mawr golf course in 1898 (Minnesota Historical Society).
Below, the Minikahda Club golf course in 1900 (Minnesota Historical Society).

The Minikahda Club and boathouse on Lake Calhoun (Minneapolis Public Library).

and L. L. Long, the building cost $15,000. In spite of the cost, additions seem to have been made frequently; a dining room being added, for example, in 1902 and new locker rooms in 1906 and 1908. Like many of the early links, the Minikahda Club course included only nine holes in 1898 but was expanded to eighteen holes by 1923. By then the sport had become immensely popular.

Individual Sports: Ice Skating, Swimming, and Jogging

Not all the sports activity on the lakes was monopolized by clubs. Many of the activities just described as club sports were enjoyed by individuals not affiliated with any club. One did not need to belong to the Lake of the Isles Driving Club to race on their course; hundreds canoed without benefit of canoe club membership; after 1916, golf was available on public courses to anyone with the fee; and membership in cycle clubs was probably not the rule for bicyclists, though accurate statistics do not survive.

Ice skating seems to have been primarily an individual sport. Speed skating clubs did exist, but the vast number of skaters who have for decades swooped around the rinks provided by the park board has not belonged to a skating club. Similarly the tobogganers, for whom a slide was built as early as 1886 at Lake Calhoun, were not organized. Since figure skating and hockey are provided for so widely across the city, it is difficult to gain any clear impression about their popularity in the district. Speed skating, however, requires a large track such as could only be provided on a frozen lake. Speed skating competitions were held regularly on Lake of the Isles during the 1920s.

The development of public bathing beaches and bathhouses was greatly slowed by the standards of public modesty that prevailed in the late nineteenth and early twentieth centuries. It was not proper for people to appear on the streets less than fully clothed, which meant that no one could swim unless he or she could change into a bathing costume somewhere close to the edge of the lake. A bathhouse was built at Lake Calhoun in 1890. Patronage was limited to men, who were offered the free use of bathing suits. Women protested and were allowed to use the facility for three hours in the morning. Still not content, they were provided with their own bathhouse in the following year. Both of these facilities were located on the east side of the lake between Thirty-second and Thirty-third streets.

A long line forms in front of the park board's new Lake Calhoun bathhouse, completed in 1912 (Minneapolis Park and Recreation Board).

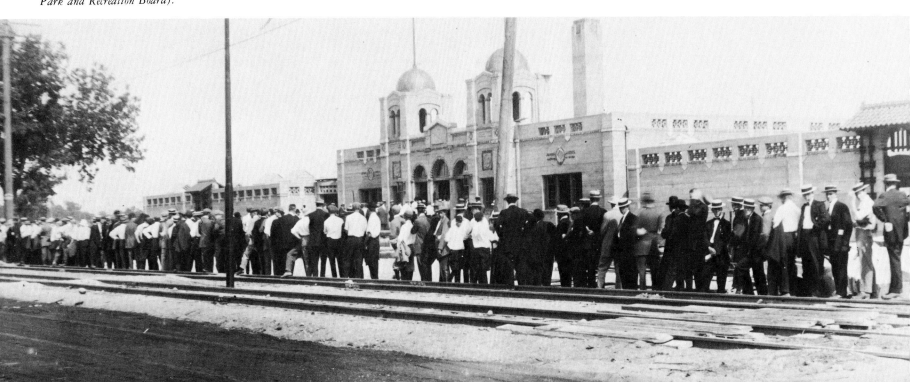

Bathers enjoying a dip in Lake Calhoun on a hot day in 1906 (Minnesota Historical Society).

Spectators outnumber bathers on the north shore of Lake Calhoun in this 1920s photo (Minneapolis Public Library).

66

After much public clamor for better facilities, a new bathhouse for both men and women was built on the north shore of Lake Calhoun in 1902. This facility became very popular, being used by 38,417 persons in 1905. At Lake Harriet, rules forbade the use of the lakeshore for bathing, except at the pavilion. At Lake Calhoun residents complained about people who came to the beach from home already dressed in their bathing suits; they asked the park board to curb the parade of "public nakedness."

The second bathhouse at Lake Calhoun was popular; but it was neither well designed nor adequate to public need. After much study, an extraordinarily elaborate bathing facility was constructed on the north shore of Lake Calhoun in 1912 for $82,000. There were 116,000 persons who used the bathhouse in the first year of its operation. However, by the 1920s, this kind of splendid facility had begun to lose favor because of the automobile. With an auto, people could travel from home to the beach in their bathing suits without causing any public outcry from the prudish. Swimming became more popular, and the bathhouse began to lose patronage.

In 1925, the beaches at Thomas and Thirty-fourth streets were officially opened to swimming, although many had been using the lakeshore for swimming previously. Lake Calhoun was the premier swimming lake for the district. The tall diving tower there was a great place for daring feats of gymnastic skill for those who did not climb back down after peeking over the edge from the second level.

In the 1970s, swimming no longer is as popular as it was in the 1930s and 1940s. The beaches are crowded with sun bathers and children, but few people are actually swimming. Gone are the diving towers and the water toboggans. In place of the swimmers one now sees the shores of the lakes crowded with joggers of every shape and style. The circle of sports fads seems to have come full circle, and we are back to our own two feet and solid ground.

Top, the water toboggan at Lake Calhoun in 1925 (Minnesota Historical Society); middle, bathers at Lake Calhoun in 1900 (Norton and Peel, Minneapolis Public Library); bottom, a floating coronation crown (Minneapolis Park and Recreation Board).

67

Workmen pose before the newly finished Lowry mansion about 1875 (Nowack, Minnesota Historical Society).

CHAPTER 5

Northern Neighborhood Tours

Lowry Hill

Lowry Hill is the wealthiest and most prestigious neighborhood in the lake district. The site of a great many impressive, well-designed mansions, this area is a favorite with tourists. **The two and one-half mile tour begins at the corner of Hennepin Avenue and Vineland Place, the location of the Walker Art Center and the Guthrie Theatre.** No residents of the neighborhood will need an introduction to these two world-famous art centers, no tourists in Minneapolis will want to miss the opportunity to see one of the Guthrie's productions and to visit the exhibits at the Walker.

Proceed south on Hennepin Avenue for one block to Groveland Terrace and turn right.

One of the most famous mansions in Minneapolis once stood on the site occupied since 1947 by the North American Life and Casualty Insurance Company. The Thomas Lowry house was built in 1874 on the outskirts of Minneapolis on the hill that was then called "the Devil's Backbone." Since Lowry and his family were the only residents there and since he owned most of the land in this neighborhood, the hill and eventually the whole area became known as Lowry Hill. Lowry's activities as a real estate developer and street railway entrepreneur have already been described on p. 20. In keeping with his

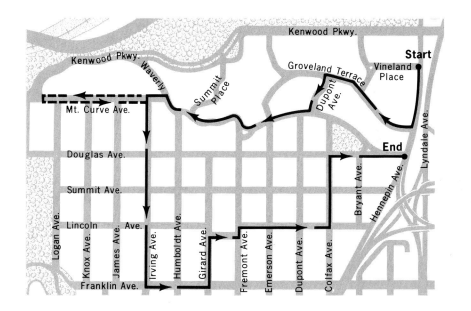

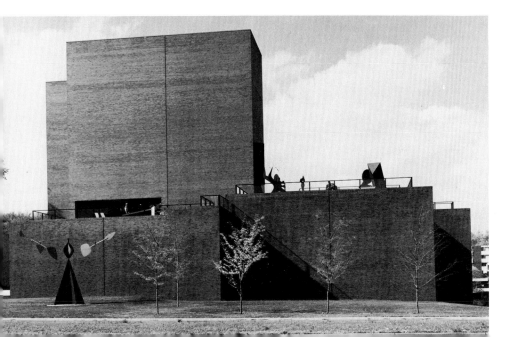

The Guthrie Theatre as it appeared when constructed
in 1963 (Guthrie Theatre).

Top left, the Walker gallery when first constructed in 1927
resembled a Moorish-Venetian palace; center left, it was given
a new facade in 1944; bottom left, the new Walker Art Center,
completed in 1971 (Walker Art Center).

business reputation, Lowry's house was a grand one, a
three-story brick Second Empire residence, topped with
the mansard roof customary for that style. The view of
the old city of Minneapolis from the bay windows and
front porch must have been magnificent. The estate occupied the entire block now enclosed by Hennepin Avenue, Groveland Terrace, Bryant Avenue, and Vineland
Place.

The Lowry family occupied the house until 1915,
when the property was purchased by Thomas B. Walker,
a wealthy lumberman who by 1915 had passed control of
the family business to his sons and was devoting himself
to his art collection. Until his move to Lowry Hill,
Walker had housed his immense collection in wings of
his residence. He now began to plan the construction of a
special gallery, which was completed at a cost of
$300,000 and opened to the public in 1927. Walker
died a few months after the opening of his new gallery,
and the old Lowry mansion was torn down in 1932.
During World War II, the gallery, which had been de-

The William L. Donaldson house, 21 Groveland Terrace, built in the 1890s in the Romanesque style (Minnesota Historical Society).

signed to resemble a Moorish-Venetian palace, was re-modelled in a style more in keeping with the emphasis the curators were then placing on modern art. The Guthrie Theatre was built in 1963 (architect, Ralph Rapson); the present Walker Art Center, designed by Edward Larrabee Barnes and built on the site of the 1927 gallery, was opened in 1971.

Proceed westward on Groveland Terrace two blocks to Dupont Avenue.

Groveland Terrace was developed as a prestigious residential street during the 1890s, gaining a good deal of its status from Thomas Lowry's beautiful estate. Two of the largest houses, the George H. Partridge mansion at One Groveland Terrace (1897) and department store magnate William L. Donaldson's house at 21 Groveland Terrace, have been razed. What survives from the 1890s is all the work of architect Frank B. Long in collaboration with various partners. The Nott house, 15 Groveland Terrace, was built in 1892 by Long and Kees; it is a dignified two and one-half story Romanesque residence. For his own house at 25 Groveland Terrace (1894), Long built a striking and interesting Richardsonian Romanesque residence, which was not originally designed with its present semi-octagonal front porch. The brick residence at 27 Groveland Terrace (1900) was designed by F. B. Long in collaboration with his son, Louis L. Long.

Turn left on Dupont Avenue, climb the hill to Mount Curve Avenue, and turn right. The tour will follow Mount Curve westward to the point where it meets Kenwood Parkway, a distance of slightly more than half a mile.

For almost a century, Mount Curve has been a much sought-after fashionable address, and, as a result, many of the older residences on the street have been razed and replaced with newer houses. In contrast to much of the rest of Lowry Hill, there is a great variety of architectural period and style along Mount Curve.

On the right side of the street at 1106 Mount Curve, where today stands a white frame rambler built in 1947, there was once the residence of the Reverend Henry Beard. This minister, who came to Minnesota for his health, seems to have been one of the earliest residents on Mount Curve, building his house in 1881. He is also said to have been responsible for the grading of the avenue. Across the street at 1101, there is a very handsome red brick residence and carriage house designed in 1895 by architect J. A. McLeod.

As you pass the intersection of Emerson, the overgrown and abandoned Dunwoody property can be seen on the right, especially the entrance gates about 200 feet south. William H. Dunwoody, one of the pioneer flour millers of Minneapolis, commissioned William Channing Whitney to build his Tudor Revival brick residence in 1905. Whitney built another very similar house in 1910 for the Horace Irvine family at 1006 Summit Avenue, Saint Paul, a house that since the 1960s has served as the official residence of the Minnesota governor. The Dunwoody mansion was razed in 1967, leaving the beautiful grounds to the squirrels, birds and inquisitive children.

On the left, across from the Dunwoody site, at 1203 Mount Curve stands an impressive red brick house designed by J. A. McLeod in 1895. The decision to turn the house forty-five degrees so that the Classical Revival portico faces the intersection has greatly augmented the appearance of the building.

After passing Fremont Avenue, one sees the Martin house (1904) at 1300 Mount Curve on the right. Like the Dunwoody house, this residence was designed by William Channing Whitney but in this case in the tradition of Beaux-Arts eclecticism, as an Italian Renaissance palace. Impressively sited on a large and well-landscaped lot, the Martin house remains the best example of the grandeur of the old Mount Curve.

Immediately to the west stand two houses designed by architect William M. Kenyon. On the south at 1315 Mount Curve there is a 1909 Early Modern Rectilinear brick residence, which shows the influence of the Prairie School in its detailing. On the north at 1314 Mount Curve, Kenyon in 1931 designed a much more traditional house in Tudor Revival style.

The Winton house at 1324 Mount Curve was built in 1910; designed by Chicago architect George W. Maher, it is an unmistakable product of the Prairie School. Maher worked in the same office as Frank Lloyd Wright and George G. Elmslie while still in his twenties, and later competed successfully against Wright for residential commissions in Oak Park and some of the other Chicago suburbs. Maher, unlike Wright, designed his houses with conservative, traditional forms but modern decorative elements such as the pair of pedestal lanterns on either side of the entryway.

To the south of the Winton house, one can see two more Tudor Revival houses from the early twentieth century at 1325 and 1415 Mount Curve. The latter was originally sited on a very large parcel of land, which later owners have subdivided and sold off. Collectively, the Dunwoody, Martin and Winton houses on the north side of Mount Curve, and 1315, 1325 and 1415 Mount Curve on the south side, display virtually the entire range of styles available to a wealthy client during the first decade of the twentieth century. For the conservative, there was the Tudor Revival style, illustrated at the Dunwoody mansion and at 1325 and 1415 Mount

A 1908 view of the gardens and west elevation of the Dunwoody mansion, with the Minneapolis skyline in the distance (Western Architect).

Curve. For the ostentatious there was the Beaux-Arts palazzo style illustrated at 1300 Mount Curve. And for the adventuresome there was the new, modern, Prairie style illustrated at 1315 and 1324 Mount Curve.

Following Summit Place around to the right only a few yards, an unusually old house can be found at number 46. Moved onto the lot in 1904, it is built in a style that can only be described as Greek Revival. It has proven impossible to date the house accurately, and it is tempting to think that it may be as old as the 1870s. However, it is probably an early 1880s house designed by a very old-fashioned carpenter.

Continuing westward, one passes a series of 1920s residences at 1418, 1500, 1505, and 1506 Mount Curve. But to the north of Mount Curve at 1520 Waverly Place, on the edge of the bluff, stands the most striking modern house in the neighborhood. This uncompromising example of the International style was built in 1970 and designed by Horty, Elving and Associates.

This Tudor Revival mansion at 1415 Mount Curve was built about 1910 (Minnesota Historical Society).

Beyond Waverly Place on the north side at 1600 Mount Curve stands the Brooks house, built by the widow of grain, lumber and banking magnate Lester R. Brooks. Designed by Edwin H. Hewitt in 1905, the Brooks house is, like the Winton house at 1324, a Prairie style version of the Renaissance palazzo. Sheathed in smooth stucco, the house is approached across a broad terrace raised five steps above the ground level. The wide doorway, a little left of center, is set in a pavilion. Over the door there is a recessed window as wide as the doorway but divided by two columns, a treatment repeated on the first floor. The most obvious Prairie School features of the design are the drip molding surrounding the window and doorway, and the two square Sullivanesque medallions above and on either side of the doorway.

Continuing to the west, there are five houses between Irving and James avenues. On the south, 1607 Mount Curve was built in 1910, 1621 Mount Curve in 1899. On the north, 1606 Mount Curve was designed for the Fess family by architect Ernest Kennedy in 1906. The Jaffray house at 1616 Mount Curve was designed by architects Sedgwick and Saxton in 1905, and its neighbor to the west at 1620 was designed by C. S. Sedgwick alone in 1895.

On the north side of Mount Curve in the 1700 block, there is an architecturally and historically fascinating group of residences. The oldest house on the block is the second in the series, 1712 Mount Curve, designed by Kees and Colburn in 1906 for L. S. Donaldson, brother and business partner of William L. Donaldson who lived on Groveland Terrace. This huge property has recently been subdivided, the modern house at 1700 being built in 1960; the architects were Bliss and Campbell. On the western edge of the property at 1720 stands a residence that was formerly the carriage house of the Donaldson estate, but which was converted to a residence in 1958 by architect Hugh Peacock. When the carriage house was sold in 1958, it was still being used as a garage for a 1923 Rolls Royce. In 1964 the house at 1716 Mount Curve was slipped in between the Donaldson residence and former carriage house.

For the remainder of the length of Mount Curve, turn-of-the-century houses alternate with contemporary dwellings until one reaches 1916, the last house on the avenue. Built in 1964 and designed by Baker-Lange Associates, this contemporary essay in the blending of house and terrain contrasts strikingly with the first and earliest house on this tour, the Lowry mansion, which was designed to be seen.

Turn around and return down Mount Curve to Irving Avenue; turn right and proceed four blocks south.

In contrast to the history of the most prestigious and best-known streets in Lowry Hill, the area south of Mount Curve and the bluff has been little rebuilt and surprisingly stable. The neighborhood stretches from Hennepin Avenue on the east to Kenwood Park on the west and from Mount Curve Avenue south to Franklin Avenue or a little further. Almost all of the housing in this area was constructed between 1895 and 1910. The most common housing type is a large two and one-half story rectilinear clapboard or stucco single-family residence.

On the first block of Irving Avenue south of Mount Curve, a mixture of building periods is represented, including the unusually old house at 1724 Irving built in 1885. But in the next three blocks, forty-one out of forty-three houses were built between 1898 and 1910. Since these houses are uniformly well-maintained and free of the deleterious effect of re-siding, Irving Avenue from Douglas to Franklin forms a mini-historical district for the study of this housing type. The principal type of alteration has been the removal of the front porches and remodelling of facades so that the houses resemble Georgian models more closely. Among the lovely and impressive houses along these blocks, notice especially 1766 with its cross-gabled gambrel roof, the brick house at 1790 that is highlighted by a giant order Corinthian portico, and one of the last houses on these blocks, 1937 Irving, which has a particularly beautiful porch.

Turn left into Franklin Avenue, go two blocks east and turn left into Girard. Go north for one block and turn right, following the jogging course of Lincoln Avenue east for four blocks to Colfax Avenue. Turn left into Colfax and go north for two blocks to Douglas Avenue.

1712 Mount Curve, built in 1906, shows Prairie School influence in its decoration (Living Historical Museum).

Architect L. A. Lamoreaux's sketch and floor plan of the residence at 1807 So. Dupont (Western Architect).

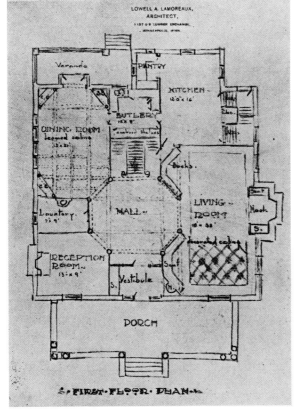

Residence at 1900 So. Dupont, photographed shortly after its construction in 1896 (Minnesota Historical Society).

As you ascend the hill on Girard, notice the unusual and distinguished stone and brick residence at 1912 Girard, built in 1889 for $6000. Turning right into Lincoln, it is possible to glimpse a side view of the houses fronting on the main north-south streets. Houses such as 1834 Fremont, still retain their enormous carriage houses.

At 1900 Dupont (the southwest corner of Lincoln and Dupont) stands a house that might be considered archetypal for this neighborhood. Built in 1896 for an estimated cost of $6000, this brick veneer residence illustrates the renewed interest in Georgian design that

Except for the missing column and pilaster capitals, this Georgian Revival residence at 905 Douglas is beautifully preserved (Living Historical Museum).

began to sweep the country in the 1890s. Although virtually every design feature of the house (from the semi-circular front porch and twin bays once topped with balustrades, to the pedimented and semi-circular dormers) is borrowed from late Georgian models, the house remains a familiar two and one-half story rectilinear dwelling with a floor plan that is anything but Georgian.

Turning left at Colfax Avenue, one passes two blocks of turn-of-the-century houses, which on the right side of the street tend to be late 1890s and on the left early twentieth century. The Georgian Revival house on the left at the northwest corner of Summit and Colfax is so large that one is astonished at it. On the right side of Colfax between Summit and Douglas, there are five last essays in the turn-of-the-century style to end this tour. At the corner, 1787 Colfax was built in 1895 by contractor T. P. Healy for $7000. The next two houses were built in 1897 for $5000 each, 1777 Colfax being designed by architect William Kenyon. William Channing

Whitney was the architect for the expensive $15,000 residence at 1775 Colfax, built in 1905. The architect for the striking corner house at 1769 Colfax (1898) is not known, but the design shows that he was able to express a much more thorough sense of the Georgian style than one usually sees in the 1890s. That the building is constructed in wood while at places pretending to be stone (at the corner quoin blocks, for example), increases its resemblance to a New England Georgian dwelling.

Turn right on Douglas and go two blocks east to return to Hennepin and the starting point for this tour.

Across the park, the modern building of the First Unitarian Society can be seen at 900 Mount Curve. On the left at the intersection of Mount Curve and Hennepin stood "Grey Court," the E. G. Walton house — built in 1893, designed by Orff and Joralemon, bought by the University Club in 1919, and razed in 1959.

The Wedge

The East Lowry Hill neighborhood (familiarly known as the Wedge), was the earliest section of the lake district to be platted and settled. South of Twenty-fifth Street the housing was interestingly varied, with small, inexpensive cottages being constructed next to elaborate, high-style dwellings. North of Twenty-fifth Street the building lots were larger and so, as a rule, were the houses. For several generations the neighborhood remained a prosperous and attractive area for people of modest means as well as affluence.

The twenty years following World War II were unkind decades for all older neighborhoods, but the Wedge suffered more than most. First of all, many well-meaning homeowners, hoping to protect their dwellings and save themselves the drudgery and expense of re-painting, fell victim to contracting companies that specialized in re-siding wooden houses with tarpaper, asbestos shingles, stucco, and (more recently) aluminum siding. Most of this re-siding obliterated the original decorative detail, altered the appearance of doorways and windows, and generally degraded the characteristic appearance of the old houses.

Secondly, the neighborhood was rezoned to allow multiple-family apartment construction. The greatest impact of this kind of new construction was felt north of Twenty-fifth Street where the larger lots attracted the interest of potential apartment building owners.

Lastly, a number of streets within the neighborhood were turned into one-way heavy-traffic thoroughfares, the quiet of the East Lowry Hill neighborhood being sacrificed to the comfort of others who wished to pass through.

This dreary saga is a much too familiar one in the history of American cities — a once pleasant neighborhood loses political influence and a sense of its own identity, is defeated in critical political battles by speculators and developers, and suddenly wakes up to find the home place uninhabitable. Usually people have sighed, shrugged, and moved on. In the 1970s, some neighborhoods like East Lowry Hill have tried to fight back.

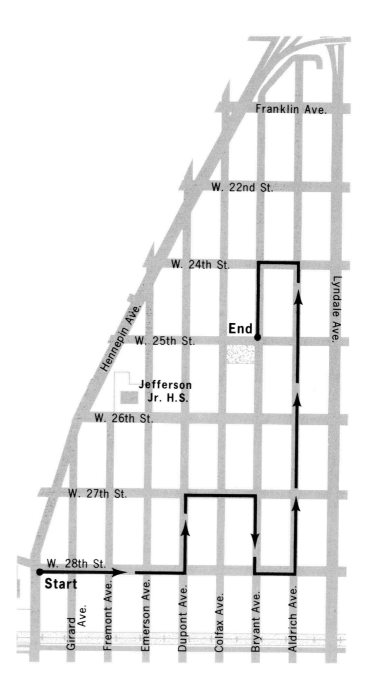

A splendid porch and proud residents at 2639 So. Bryant in 1895 (Minnesota Historical Society).

This tour is designed to explore a few of the surviving fine old houses and streetscapes in East Lowry Hill and to point out places where it is yet not too late to save others.

Start this tour by walking or driving east on West Twenty-eighth Street, beginning at the intersection of Hennepin Avenue. The tour is only about one and one-half miles long but ends at Twenty-fifth Street and South Bryant Avenue, about three-quarters of a mile from the spot where we begin.

Twenty-eighth Street is the location of many early houses, about twenty of which survive. At 1320 West Twenty-eighth (the corner of Girard) stands one of the best preserved houses in the neighborhood, one which deserves landmark designation. Since it was built before the city began to keep records in 1884, the house cannot be accurately dated, but it is undoubtedly a late 1870s or early 1880s structure. The basic outline of the house is reminiscent of Italianate styles, but the decoration is newer. The rear portion of the house seems to have been added at a later date.

Continue east on Twenty-eighth Street, keeping to the left of the one-way street. Turn left at the

stoplight into Dupont Avenue (also a one-way street.)

This block contains all of the glories and distress of this neighborhood. There are fifteen pre-1900 houses on this one block, which is remarkable. Only three out of the fifteen are in a good state of preservation and many of the houses are not even in a good state of repair, which is deplorable.

At 2742 Dupont, the builder Henry Parsons in 1895 constructed one of the most delightfully idiosyncratic Queen Anne style houses in Minneapolis. Across the street at 2735 stands a well-maintained 1887 residence. In mid-block at 2726, there is a large brick four-flat with a completely inappropriate Spanish Colonial two-story front porch. Look a little closer and you will see that this is really a much older and more interesting house than

first appeared to be the case. Built in 1887, at least a decade after this style had ceased to be fashionable, the twelve room mansion was constructed as the home of Colonel Francis Peteler, whose company, the Peteler Portable Railway Manufacturing Company, manufactured a dump car of Peteler's invention which is said to have made possible the construction of the railroads of the northwest. The colonel must have been a conservative fellow, for his house is pure Italian villa, sporting even an elegant cupola, today much in need of repair.

At 2701 Dupont, on the southeast corner, stands the earliest (1884), most expensive ($7500), and most elegant house on the block. The two and one-half story shingled Queen Anne style dwelling shows costly touches on every facade. For example, the chimney is constructed of a special brick and decorated with a terra-

A 1910 streetscape of Colfax Avenue looking north at the corner of Twenty-second (Minnesota Historical Society).

Above, 1320 East Twenty-eighth Street;
below, 2701 So. Dupont (Living Historical Museum).

cotta panel. In striking contrast, diagonally across Twenty-seventh Street there stand three originally identical 1885 houses, which cost $1750 each and were built on twenty-six foot lots.

In 1889, the horsecar route turned west into Twenty-seventh Street off Lyndale and came up to Dupont Avenue (where we are now standing.) At this intersection the route split, with some cars continuing west to Hennepin and others travelling south to Lakewood Cemetery. The small group of commercial buildings on the northeast corner is probably a survival from the days when this intersection was served by the horsecar.

Turn right on West Twenty-seventh Street and drive two blocks east. Turn right again into Bryant Avenue.

Notice the many small houses that characterize the architecture of this block. On the right side, 2724 and 2728 Bryant were built before 1885, and 2734 in 1886. Across the street, 2741 Bryant was also constructed before 1885; this is perhaps the most preserved small house in the East Lowry Hill neighborhood and serves as an excellent example of a residence that probably cost less than $1000 to build. In contrast, the last house on the right, 2752 Bryant, cost $3900 to build in 1886 and must certainly have been considered a distinguished residence by anyone in Minneapolis.

Turn left into Twenty-eighth Street (a one-way street), drive east one block, turn left again into Aldrich Avenue, and drive four blocks north.

The streetscape of Aldrich Avenue offers a contrast of the same kind just seen on Bryant. The pleasant, quiet neighborhood is dotted with many older houses, the simpler dwellings usually being found in the middle of the block with the more expensive, larger houses located on the corners. A good example of this practice is found at the intersection of Aldrich and Twenty-seventh. A house stood on the site of the Tom Sawyer Park until recently. On the other three corners there are houses that must once have been impressive. Of course, 2658 Aldrich remains a striking residence. The stone and pressed brick house was constructed in 1884; the terra-cotta panel, scalloped shingles, decorated verge boards, and pilastered chimney mark this as a house with pretensions.

Roundel and terra-cotta panel at 2658 So. Aldrich.

In the middle of the 2600 block on the right-hand side, notice the two simple workingmen's cottages located at 2621 and 2623 Aldrich — two houses, each sixteen by forty feet, wedged onto a single forty foot building lot. The dwelling at 2623 seems closest to original appearance. Both houses are severely rectilinear — virtually box-like — with a simple shed-roof porch.

The 2500 block of Aldrich was the most built-up block in East Lowry Hill prior to 1892. Thirteen houses

2741 So. Bryant, a beautifully preserved small house.

Exterior and interior photographs of architect W. B. Dunnell's residence, 2408 So. Aldrich, as it appeared about 1900 (Northwest Builder and Decorator).

earlier than that date still survive on this block, most of them being located toward the north end of the block. Unhappily, not a single well-preserved house can be found among the whole group. The asbestos and stucco siding salesmen have done their damage here; in addition, a great many two-story porches have been added to the facades of the houses.

After crossing Twenty-fifth Street, the streetscape changes decisively. There is a large newer apartment building on the left side and two flat buildings from 1911 on the right, but, after passing these multiple-family units, one can see that the houses are both larger and more recent than the majority of those we have been examining on the blocks from Twenty-eighth to Twenty-fifth Street. In contrast to the last block, there is only one house here constructed before 1890. But aside from the large apartment block, everything else dates from *c.* 1900. Lots in this section of the Wedge range from forty to sixty feet, while the lots south of Twenty-fifth Street are ordinarily forty feet or narrower, with frequent examples of subdivision within a forty-foot lot.

The historical photograph of the Dunnell house, 2408 Aldrich, provides a valuable view of the pristine appearance of the exterior of the house and a rare view of one of the principal rooms. The Dunnell house was built in 1890 for $3000. Across the street from the Dunnell house, it is interesting to survey the variety of gable-end ornament, a great deal of which survives in spite of residing.

Turn left at Twenty-sixth Street, drive one block, and turn left again into Bryant Avenue.

If you would like to make a short detour at this point in order to view a block on which some encouraging restoration is taking place, drive around to the 2100 block of Bryant, just north of Twenty-second Street (traffic barriers may make a round-the-block circuit necessary). In the 2100 block of Bryant, on both sides of the street, a group of eight or nine houses in 1978 were in various promising stages of restoration. The first six houses on the east side of the street, all built *c.* 1892 by P. C. Richardson, contain some common features such as the bowed window to the left of the main entrance.

The 2400 block of South Bryant Avenue is the most elegant and best preserved streetscape in East Lowry

The Gluek mansion, 2447 South Bryant, sketched by Robert K. Halladay (Fifth Northwestern National Bank).

Hill. Only one house out of the original twenty-three has been razed and replaced by an apartment. Very little re-siding has taken place, and most houses are in remarkably good state of repair.

With the exception of two houses built in 1910–11, all of the houses on the block were constructed between 1894 and 1906. Half of them were built by two different contractors, T. P. Healy and Henry Ingham. Thus, although there is a wide variety of decorative detail present on the block, the houses do share a basic unity of period and builder. Of great significance for the block is the fact that two of the most prestigious houses in East Lowry Hill were constructed on this block, anchoring both its north and south approaches.

The John G. Gluek house at 2447 South Bryant is undoubtedly the most famous house in the Wedge. Built in 1902 for $10,000, it was designed by architect William Kenyon for one branch of Gluek family, a name made familiar by its brewing company label. The Colonial Revival house is characterized by bold use of balustrades, but what really makes the house stand out is its beautiful siting on the triple lot.

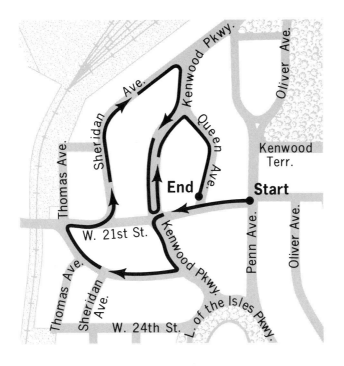

Kenwood

Kenwood is an example of a nineteenth-century, upper-middle-class suburb that has, miraculously, survived into the 1970s virtually intact. Platted by 1880, there were already three dozen residences constructed in Kenwood by 1892; most of them still survive in a good state of preservation. That Kenwood, even in the 1970s, continues to resemble a kind of sleepy rural hamlet is due to its unusual isolation. In the nineteenth century, Kenwood was cut off from the rest of Minneapolis by the railroad tracks on the north and west, by the John Green farm (since become Kenwood Park) on the east, and by the swamp south of Twenty-fourth Street. Except for the swamp, these features continue to buffer the neighborhood. Beautifully sited between Cedar Lake and Lake of the Isles, Kenwood was situated just high enough for residents to escape the mosquitoes and the malaria that the mosquitoes could carry.

The tour will begin and end at the intersection of Penn Avenue and Twenty-first Street. Since it winds through less than one and one-half miles of pleasant streets, this is an ideal walking tour, although it may be taken in an automobile as well. Before leaving the Penn Avenue intersection, notice the topography of shops and school, which gives a small-town feeling to the streetscape. And take a look, too, at the Kenwood Garage, an old-fashioned service station found virtually nowhere else in the Twin Cities.

Walk west on Twenty-first Street two blocks to the intersection of Kenwood Parkway. You will pass Queen Avenue on the right; the houses located there will be described at the end of the tour. Just past the intersection of Queen Avenue, on the left, at 2305 Twenty-first Street, is an attractive Queen Anne style dwelling (1890) sided in clapboard and shingles with a noteworthy horseshoe-shaped gable-end porch facing the street.

Turn left into Kenwood Parkway and walk one block south.

On the southwest corner at 2104 Kenwood Parkway is found a large and unusually expensive house. Built in 1892 for $15,000 and designed by E. S. Stebbins, this is a lovely exemplification of the Queen Anne style; the canopy of old oaks adds greatly to the charm of the site. Further down the block there are a number of other older houses: the Daniels house at 2112 Kenwood Parkway was built in 1890 and designed by architect Harry W. Jones; the stucco house at 2116 was built in 1887 and, like 2104, was designed by E. S. Stebbins; across the street at 2115 is an 1890 house that has lost some of its original charm. Looking down Kenwood Parkway toward Lake of the Isles and the Peavey Fountain, you can see how the land slopes toward what would have been a marshy shore in the 1890s; and perhaps you can also recognize the relative newness of the houses that have been built on those lower sections of Kenwood Parkway.

Turn right into Twenty-second Street and walk west and north as the street curves around to Twenty-first Street.

On the left at 2405 West Twenty-second Street is a Prairie style residence built in 1915. Further along on the left you will note a gracious 1890s residence: 2427

was constructed in 1898 for $3000. Across the street at 2418 is an attractively landscaped 1920s Tudor villa. At the end of the block at 2200 Sheridan Avenue is a once-splendid Queen Anne house built in 1891 for $10,000. When you reach Twenty-first Street, you will be able to see the railroad tracks on the left. In the 1890s the Kenwood commuter station was located just across the tracks, providing the fastest link with the Minneapolis business district. This railroad station made Kenwood's suburban existence possible, although streetcar connections on Douglas Avenue also supplemented the railroad's service.

Turning east into Twenty-first Street, walk one block to Sheridan Avenue.

On the right at 2505 and three houses further east at 2417 stand two 1891 Queen Anne style houses built by the same contractor, H. J. Bauman, who was also responsible in 1892 for building 2021 Sheridan, a few hundred feet up ahead. This kind of duplication — even down to the contractor — is unusual in Kenwood. Very little speculative building seems to have occurred, and virtually every house seems to have been specially built to the specifications of the owner.

Turn left into Sheridan Avenue and walk about

2104 Kenwood Parkway (Living Historical Museum).

Gable detail at 2038 Sheridan (Living Historical Museum).

one-quarter mile to the intersection with Kenwood Parkway.

Located immediately on the left at 2038 Sheridan is what probably is the oldest house in Kenwood and one of the oldest houses in the lake district. It predates the commencement of building records by the City of Minneapolis and may be as old as the 1870s. In style, certainly, it reflects the taste of the 1870s, especially the pierced brackets and gable-end motifs. The house, unfortunately, was covered with stucco at a later date. A bit further along are three more early houses — 2025–27 from 1889, 2021 from 1892, and 2026 from 1887. They have all suffered considerably from alterations over the years.

After crossing Franklin Avenue, you will notice that the railroad switching yards lie just to the west of Sheridan, a factor that has naturally affected property values. As a result, the houses are often much more modest than those we have been passing. Such smaller houses can be seen at 2004 and 1988 Sheridan, for example. Only one house on the left predates the twentieth century: 1976 Sheridan was built in 1889. At the end of Sheridan, as the ground rises and we approach Kenwood Parkway, you can notice how the size of the houses increases. At 1940 Sheridan, the dormer and gable-end windows have been given an ogee shape, which imparts a slightly Moorish effect to the house. Such ogee windows and dormers are found quite frequently in the lake district and may have been a local fad.

Turn right into Kenwood Parkway and walk down to Twenty-first Street, staying on the right side of the street.

You will retrace your steps to the intersection of Queen Avenue on the other side of the street. Kenwood Parkway is the most travelled street in this neighborhood and, not surprisingly, is the location of the largest and most impressive houses. In this block there are eight surviving 1880s houses and six from the 1890s. At 1960 Kenwood there stands an 1887 Queen Anne with a lovely design on the pediment of the porch. This house was built on a site four lots to the south and moved onto this spot in 1900. At 1968 and 1974 are two houses built in 1889.

At 2000 Kenwood stands a truly delightful house, which almost defies classification. Built in 1899 for $10,000 and designed by McLeod and Lamoreaux, the house is matched by its equally picturesque carriage house. The roof is especially high with attic vents at the fourth story level, which bear a charming resemblance to dovecotes. At 2008, 2016, and 2028 Kenwood Parkway there are three 1887 houses designed by G. W. and F. D. Orff and built by H. C. Raymond, contractor. Raymond is also listed as the builder of 1960 Kenwood Parkway. The houses are not identical, and one must strain to find similarities.

Cross Kenwood Parkway at the corner and turn back to the north.

On the open space just north of the corner house, 2035 Kenwood, the earliest schoolhouse for Kenwood was constructed in the late 1880s. The house next door was built in 1890 and was also designed by the Orff

An example of the smaller houses in Kenwood, 1988 Sheridan.

Ogee-shaped windows, such as these at 1940 Sheridan, are often found in the lake district.

An unusual roofline and interesting fleur-de-lis *set this house at* 2000 *Kenwood Parkway apart from all its neighbors.*

The Coppage house, 1912 *Queen Avenue, as it appeared when first built* (Northwest Builder and Decorator).

brothers. Both 2019 and 2015 were built about 1900. The neo-Georgian details of 2015 Kenwood indicate that the Queen Anne style had been replaced by the newer mode before the turn of the century. At 2001 and 1971 Kenwood Parkway we have an interesting comparison: the J. A. Ridgway family built a house in 1887 at the first address; eight years later Ridgway, a contractor, hired the same architect, Harry W. Jones, to build another house at 1971 Kenwood Parkway, only two lots to the north of his residence. The house at 1971 remains in excellent condition and must look today very much the way it did when first built. The central chimney stack and the detailing of the porch are noteworthy.

Walking past the house at the corner of Kenwood Parkway and Queen Avenue (a greatly altered 1897 house designed by Bertrand and Chamberlain), **turn right into Queen Avenue.**

Queen Avenue is a treasure trove of attractive residences set on perhaps the loveliest street in the neighborhood. Variety and surprise characterize the streetscape. At 1961 Queen one finds a well-preserved example of a shingle-sided rectilinear house, which one would think would have been built earlier than 1903. Next door stands an 1889 Queen Anne residence with an unusual side entrance; the architect was George E. Bertrand. Across the street at 1918 Queen, Bertrand designed another attractive Queen Anne cottage in 1889.

Harry W. Jones designed 1912 Queen Avenue for the B. R. Coppage family in 1891. The 1891 photograph shows the house before removal of its porch and before the windows in the gable-end were altered. There are three other early houses on the block — 2024 and 2030 were built in 1886, and 2029 (on the corner) was built in 1887. The Pattee house at 2029 Queen is undoubtedly the best preserved house in Kenwood. Especially noteworthy is the wide screened porch, a feature that has seldom remained intact. The colonnaded house across the street at 2036, built in 1899, seems like a modern interloper in the presence of the Pattee house, the embodiment of the old Kenwood.

1969 Queen Avenue, an attractive Queen Anne designed by George E. Bertrand.

A panoramic view of the southeastern shoreline of Lake of the Isles in about 1905 (Minneapolis Public Library).

CHAPTER 6

Southern Neighborhood Tours

Lake of the Isles

Ever since the beginning of this century, the drive around Lake of the Isles has been a popular diversion for city residents. Whether one rides in a carriage or an automobile, walks or jogs, the route around Lake of the Isles seems to capture the quintessence of landscape beauty. This tour is designed to enhance interest in the round-the-lake circuit by pointing out some of the principal architectural landmarks and providing a bit of historical background.

The tour begins on the southeast corner of Lake of the Isles just past the railroad bridge and the mall. The route to be followed is simply the counterclockwise drive around the lake on Lake of the Isles Boulevard, except for a small detour off Twenty-sixth Street to view the Purcell house.

The southeastern quadrant was the earliest settled portion of the shoreline. The first six houses on the boulevard, for example, were built around 1907. However, 2855 is the newest house on the lake, being built in 1972. At the end of the first block stand three neo-Georgian duplexes built in 1922 by Kees and Colburn.

At the end of the next block at 2801, you will see a large yellow brick residence designed by Harry W. Jones in 1910. Built almost entirely without applied decoration, the surface still presents a rich appearance due to the elaborate patterning of the brickwork. Across James Avenue at 2737, there is a pretty gambrel-roofed 1903 house built by Henry Ingham. The islands that can be seen to the left of the boulevard are maintained as wildlife sanctuaries and nesting grounds for the hundreds of wildfowl that can be seen in the lake and on the shore during warm weather.

The houses on either side of Twenty-seventh Street are among the oldest on the lakeshore, being constructed in 1887. Both have been remodelled after 1900 so that they no longer appear so old. Standing among the ancient lakeshore oaks, set further back on their lots than is customary, these are impressive residences. The next dozen houses were all constructed between 1903 and 1910, the houses on this side of Euclid Place being a few years older and a little less expensive than those on the other side of Euclid.

The Clifford House at 2601, on the corner of Twenty-sixth Street, was designed by Ernest Kennedy in 1930 and built for $67,000. A beautifully designed and crafted house, this Tudor Revival mansion exhibits the style to good advantage: the house looks as good as the day it was built, fits well onto its site, seems attractive and inviting, while at the same time reflecting the wealth and status of its owner.

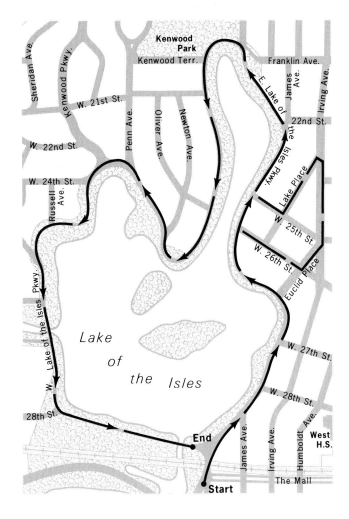

For those interested in the Prairie School tradition in Minnesota, the following six-block detour is recommended. **If you wish to skip the detour, omit the next two paragraphs. Turn right on West Twenty-sixth Street and proceed two blocks east.** On the right at 1635 is the Powers house, designed by Purcell, Feick and Elmslie in 1911.

Turn left into Euclid Place and then merge into Irving Avenue heading north. Just past Twenty-fourth Street opposite a pair of large apartment buildings, turn sharply left into Lake Place. Halfway down the block on the left at 2328 Lake Place is William Purcell's own house, built in 1913. Along the same side of the street at the corner (2424 Lake Place) is the Leslie house, built in 1917 by Long, Lamoreaux and Long. **Turn right at the corner to return to Lake of the Isles Boulevard.**

The largest and most expensive house in Minnesota history stood on the block between Twenty-sixth and Twenty-fifth streets. Designed by Chicago architects Marshall and Fox, built in 1913 for a reputed cost of $1,000,000, the Charles G. Gates mansion was not yet completed when its owner died. C. G. Gates was heir to the steel, grain and commodities fortune of speculator John W. Gates, known fondly as "bet-a-million" Gates. C. G. Gates died only a few years after his marriage, and his widow never really resided in the house.

After standing practically empty for a number of years, it was purchased in 1923 by Dr. D. F. Brooks, who, strangely enough, continued to maintain the premises but did not reside there. Possibly the building was too grand for anyone to use for so mundane an occupation as eating and sleeping. Brooks did allow charitable organizations to use the facilities for receptions and fund-raising events. After his death in 1929, the house was closed permanently and finally razed in 1933. Thus, the largest and most costly house in the state was demolished without ever being lived in. However, parts of the house were salvaged and sold off; for example, the marble staircase leading down to the game room in the Burbank-Livingston-Griggs house was obtained from the Gates mansion.

At the corner of Twenty-fifth and Lake of the Isles

Elaborately patterned brick-work enlivens the facade of 2801 East Lake of the Isles Boulevard.

Boulevard stands a house which has long been a favorite of tourists to this area. Built in 1911, designed by Frederick Soper, the building's most appealing feature is its second-story terrace and colonnade. Two doors further down the boulevard at 2409 there is a 1907 Purcell and Feick designed house. It was built before George Elmslie had joined the partnership, which may explain why the house seems to lack interest. One house to the north at 2405 stands an 1887 Queen Anne style residence with a grand front bay. Although first-story awnings and an anachronistic portico detract from the effect, this remains the most impressive nineteenth-century house on the lakeshore.

Follow the boulevard around the narrow bay to the west side of the lake and begin the western half of this circuit.

On this route you will pass the two churches along the lakeshore, Saint Paul's Episcopal Church on the right at the top of the lake and Lake of the Isles Lutheran Church on the corner of Twenty-first Street on the west side of the lake.

Aside from the first house on West Lake of the Isles Boulevard, 2002, there are no nineteenth-century houses on this side of the lake. Travelling south along the west shore of the bay, you will pass houses equally divided between the pre-World War I era and the 1920s. Notice the attractive shingled 1901 house at 2120 and the Republic of Columbia consulate at 2218. Just before the boulevard turns west, there is a striking 1910 Tudor Revival villa at 2296, its portico decorated with carved verge boards.

Look to the right as you pass Newton Avenue to catch a glimpse of the Owre house (2625 Newton), designed by Purcell, Feick and Elmslie in 1911. After crossing Newton Avenue, notice the white frame residence at 2350, the Allyn K. Ford house. Built in 1928 and reputedly designed by Ford's brother-in-law, C. W. Bazier, it is virtually the twin of the 1919 Lindsay-Weyerhaeuser house at 294 Summit Avenue, Saint Paul.

After passing the Peavey Fountain at the intersection of Kenwood Parkway, you will see the picturesque, romantic Amsden house, designed with its imitation thatched roof in 1922 by Liebenberg, Kaplan and Martin (2388

The Purcell house, 2328 Lake Place (Minneapolis Public Library).

The extravagant Gates mansion once stood on Lake of the Isles Boulevard but was razed in 1933 (Minnesota Historical Society).

95

Minneapolis, Minn., Lake of the Isles Boulevard.

Photo Copyright by Sweet, Minneapolis.

Top left, a 1908 postcard shows Peavey Fountain and Lake of the Isles Boulevard (Minnesota Historical Society);
top right, 2296 West Lake of the Isles Boulevard; below, 2388 West Lake of the Isles Boulevard.

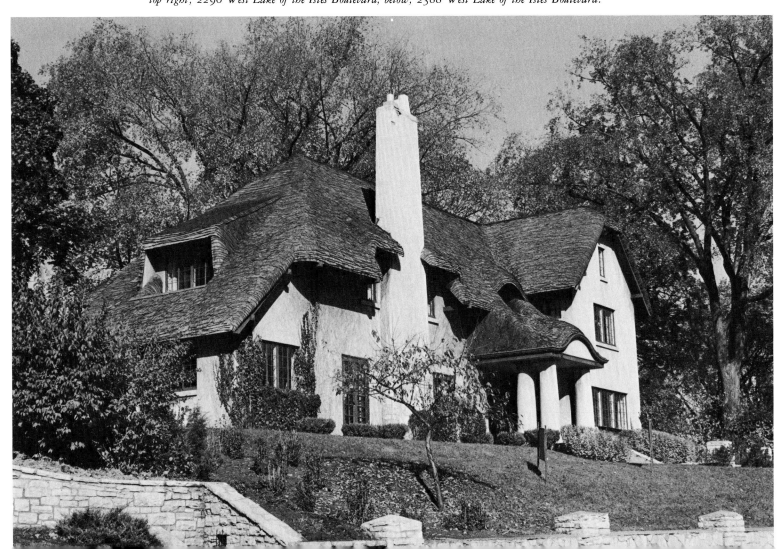

96

Lake of the Isles Boulevard). On the next corner, at 2424, there is another fine example of the Tudor Revival villa, built in 1929 and designed by Carl A. Gage. The picturesque massing of the house is slowly revealed as the road curves around the house, displaying each of its facades in turn.

At Sheridan Avenue, the boulevard becomes a two-way street continuing across the bridge over Kenilworth Lagoon. The area covered by the lagoon's water was a dismal swamp before dredging. The bridge and lagoon are a part of the linking of the lakes project that the park board completed in 1911.

Four houses south of the bridge, at 2740, there stands another house designed by Carl A. Gage. In this 1917 residence Gage created a brick and stucco essay in Georgian Revival, with a fine stone and brick entrance pavilion. The landscaping and steps contribute greatly to the effect of this house.

Continue driving around the southern shore of the lake until you cross the bridge over the channel connecting Lake Calhoun and Lake of the Isles; you will then have completed the promenade around the Lake of the Isles.

East Calhoun

This tour of the East Calhoun neighborhood will pass through an attractive part of the lake district, but the emphasis will not be placed upon the refreshing lakeshore or the pleasant residential streets. Rather, this tour is designed to emphasize transformations — to point out and isolate the interesting and instructive relics of the past that can so easily be ignored in a familiar landscape.

The tour begins at Hennepin and Lake and ends at East Calhoun Boulevard and Lake Street. A little more than two miles long, it is designed to be enjoyed from an automobile, but it is not too strenuous for walking or biking. Basically the tour will take you (via a circuitous route) from Lake Street to Thirty-sixth Street and back. Start the tour by heading south on Hennepin Avenue.

The Hennepin-Lake business district is the embodiment of transformation, but there the changes are so complete that it is difficult to find any evidence of the past. But as you pass along Hennepin from Thirty-first

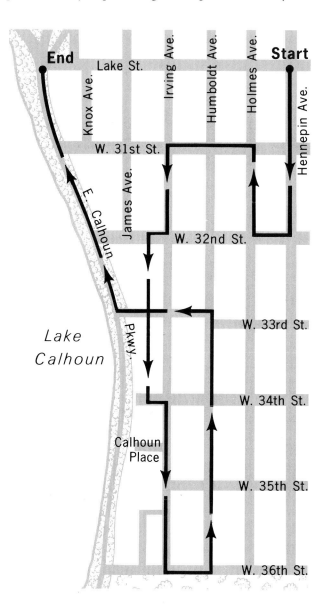

The beautiful and well-preserved porch at 3112 Hennepin Avenue.

(in spite of its asbestos siding) the character of the 1870s. The front porch, gable-end, and eaves treatment are exceptional for Minneapolis. The first house (3106–8 Hennepin), designed as a duplex, had by 1978 become the Gestalt Center. The third house, 3116 Hennepin, has been altered by the addition of a double front porch supported by giant order Ionic columns; its use has been changed from residence to church.

As you continue down the block, notice how much change is visible in the block. The large apartment units at 3120, 3121 and 3128 Hennepin have replaced older single-family dwellings. Some of the old houses are still standing, but just barely standing, looking as though they may be tomorrow's victims of progress. The most ironic scene in the block is the headquarters of Design World at 3131 Hennepin, where a company ostensibly devoted to home improvement has attached a storefront of no particular merit to a house of real character. Toward the end of the block, note the 1931 Art Deco office building at 3142 and 3146 Hennepin.

Turn right at Thirty-second Street, drive one block west, turn right into Holmes Avenue and return to Thirty-first Street.

On the corner on the left-hand side at 3100 Holmes, stands a rather nice Queen Anne style house built in 1899 for the remarkably low sum of $1800. **Turn left at Thirty-first Street, drive two blocks west, turn left into Irving Avenue and go south to Thirty-second Street.**

At this point in the tour, we are going to retrace the curious route of the old Minneapolis, Lyndale, and Minnetonka Railway, later to become the route of the streetcar that ran out to Lake Harriet (the streetcar that still runs on a shortline from Lake Harriet to the foot of Thirty-sixth Street). On its run from downtown Minneapolis, the train or trolley would head west on Thirty-first until it reached Irving and then turn left in front of Cramer Electric Company, cross Irving, and run right through the property on the west side of Irving Avenue until it reached the alley. As you approach Irving, travelling west on Thirty-first Street, you can still recognize the line of the tracks in the strange setback near Cramer Electric, and in the raised portion of Irving Avenue.

to Thirty-second Street, notice the surviving single-family dwellings, relics from the day when Hennepin was the edge of settlement and considered primarily an elegant residential boulevard. The three houses at 3106–08, 3112 and 3116 are worth stopping to examine. The house in the middle of the group must rank as one of ten most architecturally significant buildings in the lake district. Although it was built in 1887, it was designed in the style of a former era and preserves

Driving along the 3100 block of Irving, you will see that the oldest houses were built during 1900–10. At 3111 Irving, for example, there is a 1908 duplex with giant order columns supporting the double front porch. This is a characteristic house for the lake district. Further along at 3121 and 3125 Irving there are two nicely maintained examples of early twentieth-century housing. The block as a whole shows many signs of restoration.

At the corner of Thirty-second Street, turn right, go one-half block, turn left into the alley between Irving and East Calhoun Parkway, and drive two blocks south.

Along this alley you will be driving in the right-of-way for the train or trolley. Most of the alleys in this neighborhood are only twelve feet wide, but this one is much wider — thirty-three feet wide. When you come to Thirty-fourth Street, the alley will bend slightly to the right before it ends. You may be able to guess that at this point the tracks once cut over to East Calhoun Boulevard, since the train could not climb the hill immediately ahead. The house directly ahead at 3401 East Calhoun has, of course, been built since the tracks were abandoned.

In the 1870s and 80s there was a station here. As long as the Lyndale Hotel was in operation, this would have been the spot at which to get off in order to enjoy its facilities; indeed, for a short time the line ended here. Later, after the hotel had been torn down, there was a pavilion at Thirty-fourth Street that partially took the place of the Lyndale. By 1900, although the streetcar still stopped at Thirty-fourth Street, there was no longer a station or a pavilion.

After exiting from the alley at Thirty-fourth Street, turn left and drive one-half block to Irving Avenue. Turn right and drive south for two blocks to Thirty-sixth Street.

The 3400 block of Irving includes a picturesque mixture of the old and the new. On the left at 3409 is a 1901 dwelling built on the alley; such houses were sometimes constructed with the idea of later building a larger house on the front of the lot. On the west side of the street at 3408, 3412 and 3416 are a series of well-maintained turn-of-the-century houses. But at 3427 there is an unusual 1936 Art Moderne version of the Mediterranean

St. Mary's Greek Orthodox Church built in 1957 (Living Historical Museum).

The Forman mansion, built about 1900, occupied the site on which St. Mary's Greek Orthodox Church now stands (Minneapolis Public Library).

Historic photographs of two of the main rooms of the
Forman mansion (Minneapolis Public Library).

villa, followed by a series of post-World War II residences.

As you approach Thirty-fifth Street, you cannot help but notice the impressive Saint Mary's Greek Orthodox Church built in 1957, designed by Thorshov and Cerny. The site has witnessed more transformations than any other in the lake district. Location of the earliest European structure, the Pond brothers' cabin (see p. 7), it later became the site of the Lyndale Hotel pictured on p. 16. After the demolition of the hotel in the 1880s, the site remained vacant until the construction of the Forman mansion about 1900. The Classical Revival house was in turn demolished in 1955, and, after many years of indecision, the property was sold to the congregation of Saint Mary's. The cycle of transformations is almost unbelievable: pioneer cabin, resort hotel, neo-classical mansion, Greek Orthodox church.

The 3500 block of Irving contains a large group of houses from the 1930s, especially the west side of the street where there are seven residences from 1931 and 1932, all built by the same contractor, Hull-Berg, Inc.

Turn left into Thirty-sixth Street. Before you turn you can take in a very pretty view of Lake Calhoun to the west. **After one block, turn left again into Humboldt Avenue and drive north for three blocks.**

The house on the northwest corner, 3553 Humboldt, was moved onto this lot in 1911 from 1401 West Thirty-sixth Street. That address is now located within Lakewood Cemetery. Before 1900 the cemetery extended east only as far as Hennepin Avenue, the area from Hennepin to King's Highway being platted for residential use. About ten houses had been constructed in the area when the cemetery was extended to its present limits. Most of them, like 3553 Humboldt, were moved into this area.

The 3500 block of Humboldt was built one side at a time. Almost every house on the east side of the street was constructed in the decade before World War I, and all of the houses on the west side of the street were built between 1924 and 1928. In the next block there are several post-World War II houses on the left, including a very late (1945) Art Deco house at 3424 Humboldt, while the houses on the right (east) are much earlier. A simple

1920s chic: a Cadillac and fur coat on Calhoun Boulevard (Minnesota Historical Society).

turn-of-the-century cottage stands at 3401 Humboldt; it was built in 1903 for $2,000.

Toward the end of the next block on the west side of the street there is a set of row houses at 3310–20 Humboldt. Listed in the city's building records as "tenements," the five units were constructed in 1884, and, according to Theodore Wirth, they were used as a hotel for the trainmen on the Minneapolis, Lyndale and Minnetonka Railroad. The house on the northwest corner of Thirty-third and Humboldt (3246 South Humboldt) was constructed at the same time by the same company and is described at the time of its construction as a "double tenement."

Turn left at the corner of Thirty-third Street and drive two blocks west to East Calhoun Boulevard. Turn right and follow the boulevard north to Lake Street.

The earliest continuous group of lakeside residences in the district was built on this three block section of East Calhoun Parkway. The reason for this is plain if one glances to the left at the lake, for the shoreline here is about fifteen feet below the level of the roadway. Unfortunately, the houses in this section of the boulevard have not generally been well-preserved and the streetscape is difficult to interpret. The first house in the block (3247 East Calhoun) is a well-preserved brownstone and gives a clear impression of the character of buildings that were

being constructed early in the twentieth century. The dwelling at 3217 East Calhoun is the oldest on the block, being built in 1895.

In the next block was found the heaviest concentration of older houses, ten residences having been constructed before 1902, six of which are still standing. The fourth house from the corner, 3139 East Calhoun, is the best preserved house on the block. Built in 1886, this clapboard residence still expresses a certain simple dignity in the face of the transformations that have occurred around it. Two doors down the street, 3131 East Calhoun, although one year older than its near neighbor, completely belies its age; this house has twice suffered fires and subsequent rebuilding. The Queen Anne house next to it, 3125 East Calhoun, contains ogee-arched windows in its dormers, a window found frequently in the lake district.

The first three houses in the next block are all pre-1900. The apartment at 3033 East Calhoun was built in 1973 and is attractively designed for its location. At the end of the block stands the park board concession and boat rental stand on the left where the Lurline Boat Club boathouse once stood. Where the Veterans of Foreign Wars post now stands, one of the old resort hotels was constructed in 1884, a building once used as the headquarters for the Calhoun Yacht Club.

Cottage City

Facing the south shore of Lake Calhoun is a small community unlike any other in the lake district. Usually thought of as a part of the attractive Linden Hills neighborhood, it carries the stamp of history on its landscape and does not quite resemble the rest of the neighborhood. The Cottage City subdivision, stretching south from the lake to Fortieth Street and west from Richfield Road to Xerxes Avenue, was laid out in tiny twenty-five foot lots with the expectation, expressed in its name, that the smallest and simplest houses would be built there.

Very few nineteenth-century houses were built, although there were a few right on Calhoun Boulevard. The area was not built up until after the turn of the century, long after Louis Menage, the developer who platted the area, had disappeared from Minneapolis. What imparts such charm and interest to Cottage City is the variety of small houses that still dot the streets. Whether they were all built as summer cottages we do not know, but many certainly were. For example, the city building permit for 3715 and 3717 South Vincent (houses now razed) describes the two 18 × 24 foot frame structures as "summer cottages." They were each built in a month during the spring of 1904 for $350.

The Cottage City tour begins and ends on East Calhoun Boulevard and Richfield Road. A little more than a mile in length, it makes a pleasant walking tour; cars can be left in the beach parking lot at the foot of Upton Avenue. Proceeding south on East Calhoun Boulevard, continue for two blocks on the boulevard past the junction with Richfield Road on the left, following the Lake Calhoun shoreline.

In the first block on the left once stood the Ueland homestead where a series of modern dwellings have now been built. The Ueland family were among the pioneer residents of Cottage City. Andreas Ueland was a successful first generation Norwegian immigrant who built up a respected legal practice and was a charter member of the Minikahda Club. His daughter Brenda's recollections of

The Andreas Ueland house, viewed from Richfield Road looking west (courtesy of Margaret Ueland).

3715 South Thomas Avenue (Living Historical Museum).

this neighborhood capture a great deal of the special flavor of Cottage City:

> When we drove downtown, we went down our long dirt driveway to Richfield Road and then turned into the pretty boulevard that led around the lake . . . We wheeled slowly down the drive. Mother had to tell me again to be careful not to stick my legs out and touch the wheel, because it was not safe. . . .
>
> Now just where the boulevard came to our land and had to turn off toward Lake Harriet, there was the Big Rock — that is, it was about as big as a trunk — and here there was an open sandy beach with yellow sunbeams moving in dancing network under the water.

> We would drive Lady and the carriage right into the water, and she would put her head down and dawdlingly drink, or pretend to drink, looking up at the horizon after soaking her nose in it, the water sluicing out around the bit. "Oh, she has had enough. She is just fooling," we would say tenderly, and wheel in the water (look! it comes way up to the hubs!) and drive out and on our way again.

Pass Sheridan Avenue and turn sharply left into Thomas Avenue.

One's first impression of the Cottage City streetscape is deceiving. On the right are relatively large and modern

103

houses. On the left there are a series of attractive houses that only seem different on second glance. The first house on the left was built before 1884 and was probably constructed in the very early 1880s. It was undoubtedly built by a local carpenter; the original central section of the house is constructed in an old-fashioned Greek Revival style. The next house at 3715 Thomas is sited right next to the sidewalk, while its neighbor, formerly a carriage house, is located far back off the street.

As you pass Thirty-eighth Street, the streetscape changes and the first of the characteristic small houses appears. On the left, 3807 Thomas was built in 1889 for $200; it is not only one of the earliest houses but also one of the most attractive. Beginning at 3813 and following

The Cottage City streetcar stop, sketched by Robert K. Halladay. (Fifth Northwestern National Bank).

These two beautifully preserved cottages have been joined to form a single dwelling at 2617 Fortieth Street.

southward, you will see a series of five cottages that must originally have been identical. All have been altered and added to, but 3823 preserves the original simple clapboard facade. Built about 1904, these houses each cost about $500. At 3828 and 3833 the houses have been sited far back on their lots.

Turn left at Thirty-ninth Street and walk two blocks east to Richfield Road. Turn right, walking along William Berry Park for one block, and turn right into Fortieth Street.

Directly east across the park is the old streetcar line whose route was traced in the East Calhoun tour. As the car left the Thirty-fourth Street stop, old residents remember, the conductors would call out "Cottage City, next stop;" the streetcar stopped at the bridge just east of here, allowing riders to walk east to Lakewood Cemetery or west to this settlement.

Walk three blocks west to Upton Avenue. Along the south side of Fortieth Street are found examples of the smallest houses in Cottage City. At 2521 Fortieth, for example, you can see a tiny house constructed in 1902 for $350. In the middle of the next block at 2617, there are two lovely cottages built in 1902, but joined together to form a single dwelling in 1972.

Turn right into Upton Avenue and walk one block north.

The streetscape here is a mixture of old and new houses with an old store surviving on the left. At the turn of the century the park board gave serious consideration to dredging out the area west of Upton Avenue all the way to Xerxes to form a lagoon similar to the Kenilworth Lagoon on Lake of the Isles.

Turn left on Thirty-ninth Street, walk one block west, turn right into Vincent Avenue, and walk north to Lake Calhoun.

On the left side of Vincent, there is a series of turn-of-the-century houses. The second, third and fourth houses were apparently priced with close attention to the square footage involved: 3840 Vincent (18 × 20 feet) cost $400, 3836 (20 × 22 feet) cost $500, and 3832 (24 × 24 feet) cost $600.

Turn right at the intersection of West Calhoun Boulevard to return to your starting point.

Lakewood Cemetery

Passing through the entrance to Lakewood Cemetery, one enters a truly historic landscape. This special place was set aside over a century ago to serve as a last resting place and monument for the leading citizens of Minneapolis. Unlike Europeans, we have built our neighborhoods and commercial districts without leaving room for monuments. We have, instead, concentrated our permanent expressions of honor and love in the sentimental landscapes of cemeteries. Here the record of a city's history is opened for the most casual visitor to read and ponder.

When Colonel William S. King, Dr. C. G. Goodrich, W. D. Washburn, Thomas Lowry, and others combined to form the Lakewood Cemetery Association in 1871, they were following a fashion begun some fifty years earlier in Massachusetts — a fashion for elaborate suburban memorial parks separated from churchyards. On the 128 acres of land they purchased from the King Farm, they intended to establish a new place for the interment of the dead secured "on some of the beautiful locations out near the lakes, where the encroachments of the city would never seriously interfere."

The initial plan was drawn by C. W. Falsom, then superintendent of Mount Auburn, Boston, the country's most famous cemetery. However, the directors were not happy with this plan and rebuilt the cemetery as a park following the plan of Adolph Strauch, designer of Spring Hill in Cincinnati, another famous cemetery.

Lakewood epitomizes the best of romantic Victorian design. Carriage ways were laid out in gentle curves, trees and shrubs were planted so as to provide visitors with secluded glades as well as sweeping vistas. Unlike the simple markers used in older graveyards, Victorian monuments were grand and lavish. Obelisks, Greek temples, pulpits, and scrolls were all common. Human figures were used upon occasion. Epitaphs in the early 1880s were frequently flowery and listed earthly accomplishments.

Epitaphs soon went out of fashion, however. After the turn of the century, forms became more simple.

The original Thirty-sixth Street entrance to Lakewood Cemetery (Art Works of Minneapolis).

Tombstones became considerably smaller and in the modern period were designed to be flush with the ground. Unfortunately, they seldom tell much of the life of the person they represent.

In the late nineteenth century, cemeteries were considered much more than sanitary places to bury the dead. Lakewood was perceived as a beautiful addition to the Minneapolis park system. An early historian wrote:

> Thus was obtained this beautiful tract of land, with graceful rolling surface and modest oaks, touching two of the most cherished and attractive lakes, appropriately fitting into our extensive and prided park system, easy of access, and, as it were, intended by nature herself for a 'City of the Dead.' . . . Minneapolis takes pride in

the vast system of public parks and this (is) the only really public cemetery.

Lakewood was so popular that many bodies were removed from other Minneapolis cemeteries and reburied here accounting for many of the monuments and gravestones dated earlier than Lakewood's beginning. As Lakewood expanded, homes located in the southwest corner of the cemetery were moved into the Carag and East Calhoun neighborhoods.

The original gate to Lakewood Cemetery was a magnificent structure of granite, built in Romanesque style with groined arch ceilings of stone and brick. Windows in the gateway were of special design with emblems of the lotus flower, the cross, love birds, olive branches,

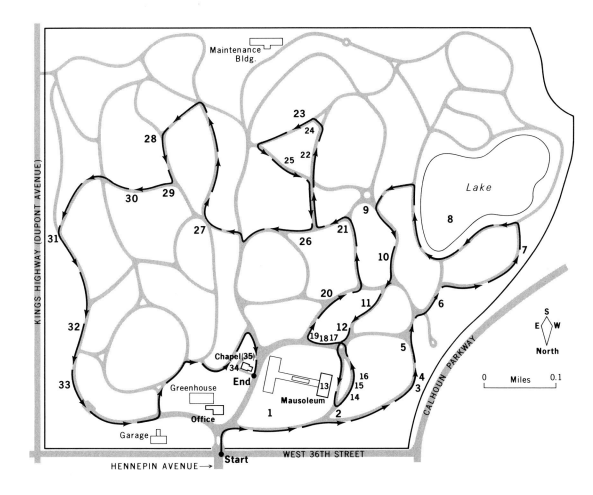

and the passion flower. Frank E. Read was the architect of the gateway, erected in 1889 at a cost of $35,000. The gateway included the cemetery offices and also an underground vault.

After passing the present gateway located at Hennepin Avenue and Thirty-sixth Street, the first monument to the right is the Thomas B. Walker memorial (1). Walker, a wealthy businessman in the sawmill business was responsible for Minneapolis' first free public art gallery, opened in 1873 (see p. 70).

Passing to the right of Fridley's monument (2), one sees the Francis memorial (3) built in 1893, one of the older monuments in Lakewood. Sir Joseph Francis was the father of the United States Life Saving Service. Next to the Francis monument is the mill explosion memorial

(4) erected in 1885 to commemorate the disaster of May 2, 1878. Unique carvings on the memorial include a bevel gear with a broken tooth. Only a simple tablet marks the actual location of the catastrophe.

Maggie Menzel (5) was the first person buried at Lakewood Cemetery. Her stone depicts a romantic, Victorian vision of a woman clinging to a cross.

The site of a second cemetery gateway is located near Lake Calhoun. Around the turn of the century the old Motor Line streetcar ran along Lake Calhoun and made a stop at this gateway depositing mourners, visitors, and even picnickers who would come to enjoy Lakewood's park-like atmosphere (6).

The next site (7) is Babyland, an area reserved exclusively for babies' graves, surrounding a statue of Jesus. Nearby is the cemetery's own small lake (8) a typical feature in the landscape of late nineteenth-century suburbs.

Many associations are represented at Lakewood including the Elks (9) who are memorialized with a giant sculptured elk, and the Quakers who have characteristically chosen modest headstones (10). An unusual grave marker is to be found next: a sculpture of a sleeping baby resting in the bottom of an upright clamshell (11). Among other historic figures buried at Lakewood is Mary Stevens (12) who was the first white child born in Minneapolis.

The next three monuments are memorials to three powerful and prominent early citizens of Minneapolis. W. L. Donaldson was a retailer who founded the great department store that bears his name today. Pillsbury's vast milling interests are symbolized on his memorial by a bundle of grain carved on the side. The fifty-foot McNair monument memorializes a prominent lawyer and developer of the lake district.

Charles M. Loring's monument (18) has the inscription "Father of the Parks." Loring was instrumental in the establishment of the first parks in Minneapolis. His memorial is flanked by two impressive monuments, those of Wolford (17) and J. W. Pence (19), which are two of the largest and most expensive memorials built in Lakewood's early history. The statuary on top of Pence's monument is a work by Caribilli. J. W. Pence was a financier who built the Pence Opera House on the corner of Hennepin Avenue and Second Street, an elegant theater opened in 1867.

On the next site (20) is located another unusually carved monument depicting the stump of a tree with an inscription carved on the side where the bark is peeled away. Further on is another organizational memorial, the Oddfellows marker.

The next two sites are the graves of well-known Minnesota figures. Floyd B. Olson (22) was the first farmer-labor governor of Minnesota, elected in 1931. William H. Dunwoody (23) was a leader in the milling industry. He bequeathed $2 million for the building and endowment of the William Hood Dunwoody Industrial Institute.

Several impressive private mausoleums are located nearby (24 and 25). The Wood mausoleum is a small pyramid and McKnight's and Fitchette's mausoleums are small temples. Continuing past the Grand Army of the Republic's monument commemorating Civil War soldiers and another association memorial, the Showmen's Rest, is the Rocheleau monument, the tallest monument in Lakewood Cemetery.

The Lowry-Goodrich (30) mausoleum marks an area of many impressive mausoleums. Thomas Lowry was the father of the Twin Cities' streetcar system and a leading developer of this area. His wife, Beatrice Goodrich, came from a family who were prominent landholders in the Lowry Hill area.

A view of the park board's equipment storage building marks the site of Colonel King's Lyndale Farm and the street on that side of the cemetery is known as King's Highway. A new memorial garden is located nearby (32) and includes a negative relief carving of Jesus. United States Senator Hubert H. Humphrey's grave (33) has a modest headstone and is marked by American flags.

The impressive Lakewood Memorial Chapel can be viewed from both back and front (34 and 35). Harry W. Jones, its architect, was associated with architect H. H. Richardson in Boston before coming to Minnesota. He also taught architecture at the University of Minnesota. Jones was responsible for many other Minneapolis structures, including the Butler brothers warehouse, the old Cream of Wheat building, and many Kenwood homes. This memorial chapel has Byzantine-inspired design and contains one of the largest true mosaics in the western world.

Notes and Acknowledgements

Notes

The most important evidence for this study has been primary sources, such as city building permits and original plat maps now located in the Minneapolis City Hall. We have also used city directories, especially for commercial and religious developments. The pamphlet and clipping files of the Minneapolis Historical Collection in the Minneapolis Public Library and the files of the Hennepin County Historical Society have proven very valuable. Historic photographs and oral history interviews have also been used to reconstruct the history of the neighborhoods. The best secondary sources for this area and period are Isaac Atwater, *History of the City of Minneapolis* (New York: Munsell and Co., 1893), and Theodore Wirth, *The Minneapolis Park System, 1883–1944* (Minneapolis, Board of Park Commissioners, 1945). Sources for quotes in the text will be found below.

6   Donald D. Parker (ed.), *The Recollections of Philander Prescott* (Lincoln: University of Nebraska Press, 1966), p. 126.

7–8   Collection of Pond papers, Minnesota Historical Society.

16   The description of the Lyndale Hotel is taken from the *Northwestern Tourist*, June 23, 1883, p. 11.

17   The description of the gala opening of the Lyndale Hotel is taken from the *Northwestern Tourist*, August 11, 1883, p. 7.

26   Wirth, *The Minneapolis Park System*, p. 19.

27   Wirth, *The Minneapolis Park System*, p. 29.

29   Wirth, *The Minneapolis Park System*, p. 91.

31   Atwater, *History of the City of Minneapolis*, p. 888.

34–35   Henry L. Griffith, *Minneapolis, The New Sawdust Town* (Minneapolis: Bolger Publishing Co., 1968), p. 28–29.

49   Brenda Ueland, *Me* (New York: Putnam and Sons, 1939), p. 33.

49–51   The quotes referring to Lake Calhoun come from Atwater, p. 72–73.

51   Thoreau's notes of his journey to Minnesota have been published by Walter Harding (ed.). *Thoreau's Minnesota Journey* (Genesco, N. Y.: Thoreau Society Booklet #16, 1962).

52   Henry David Thoreau, *The Variorum Walden* (New York: Washington Square Press, 1967), p. 222.

54   Wirth, *The Minneapolis Park System*, p. 95.

59   Wirth, *The Minneapolis Park System*, p. 231.

60–62   Robert M. Irving and Kenneth Carley "Horse Racing on Ice Was Popular in the Twin Cities," *Minnesota History* 41 (Winter 1969): 372–84, quotes from 373 and 380.

94   Information relating to the Gates mansion is found in *The Gates Mansion, a History and a Description* (Minneapolis: Japs-Olson Co., [1933]), a copy of which is located in the library of the Hennepin County Historical Society.

102–3   Ueland, *Me*, p. 23–25.

105–6   Atwater, *History of the City of Minneapolis*, p. 951.

Acknowledgements

The idea for this book was born in January 1978, during the first session of a Macalester College symposium on planning and managing the city. Having heard one of the speakers extoll the importance of *genius loci*, "the spirit of a place," John Cochran, president of the Fifth Northwestern National Bank, asked the authors if they would be willing to write a book that might help residents of the Calhoun-Isles community develop such a sense of place. During the past few decades, bankers have sometimes been attacked for low sensitivity toward issues of neighborhood preservation. If John Cochran could serve as the example, their reputation would improve dramatically; he has shown an admirable capacity for serving his community.

During the summer and early autumn of 1978, our two able research assistants, Valerie Stetson and Barbara Young, conducted a systematic inventory of documentary and photographic resources. The book owes a great deal to their skill and perseverance. They mined the collections of libraries and civic repositories for the most important primary and secondary materials. They were aided by archivists and librarians of real helpfulness. We would like to thank, especially, Ruth Zalusky Thorstenson of the Hennepin County Historical Society and Dorothy M. Burke of the Minneapolis History Collection, Minneapolis Public Library.

Part of the pleasure of writing this book has stemmed from the delight with which it has been awaited by residents of the neighborhoods. Many have helped us with suggestions, references, a glass of lemonade, or a story of the old days. Although their names are too numerous to list, we do feel a special need to express our appreciation to Sandy and Mary Hill, Anders and Trilby Christiansen, and Gladys Pattee.

Bonnie Richter has served ably as manuscript and photography editor for this project. The map on p. 2 was drawn by Pat Simmons; the eight other maps were drawn by Sandra Haas, University of Minnesota Cartographic Laboratory. Robert N. Taylor designed the book, contributing his usual good sense and insight. Irv Kreidberg and the staff at North Central Publishing Company have cooperated to help produce a beautiful book. Lastly we would like to thank our families, especially Karen and Eunice.

Index